SIMPLY ORGANIZED

*

The all-in-one guide to organizing your home, office, children, and more!

Iyna Bort Caruso and Jenny Schroedel

Adamsmedia
Avon, Massachusetts

Published by
Adams Media, a division of F+W Media, Inc.
57 Littlefield Street, Avon, MA 02322. U.S.A.
www.adamsmedia.com

ISBN 10: 1-4405-1108-X
ISBN 13: 978-1-4405-1108-0

Printed in China.

10 9 8 7 6 5 4 3 2 1

Contains material adapted and abridged from The Everything® Home Storage
Solutions Book by Iyna Bort Caruso, copyright © 2007 by F+W Media, Inc.,
ISBN 10: 1-59337-662-6, ISBN 13: 978-1-59337-662-8 and The Everything®
Organize Your Home Book, 2nd Edition by Jenny Schroedel, copyright © 2007,
2002 by F+W Media, Inc., ISBN 10: 1-59869-393-X, ISBN 13: 978-1-59869-
393-5.

This publication is designed to provide accurate and authoritative information
with regard to the subject matter covered. It is sold with the understanding
that the publisher is not engaged in rendering legal, accounting, or other
professional advice. If legal advice or other expert assistance is required, the
services of a competent professional person should be sought.
    —From a *Declaration of Principles* jointly adopted by a Committee of the
    American Bar Association and a Committee of Publishers and Associations

Many of the designations used by manufacturers and sellers to distinguish
their product are claimed as trademarks. Where those designations appear in
this book and Adams Media was aware of a trademark claim, the designations have been printed with initial capital letters.

Contents

Introduction

What's your breaking point? When do the piles of paper get so high, the old exercise bicycle in the basement so dusty, the toys in the playroom so trip-worthy that you reach the end of your rope?

Everyone's got a story, and there are no urban legends among them. There's the businessman whose slim closet couldn't fit another item. Rather than sort through his clothes and get rid of his never-wears, he came up with an ingenious solution—or so he thought. You decide. He hung his excess shirts off ceiling fans throughout his home.

The tales of an exasperated spouse going to extreme measures are endless. Many are variations on the "while you were out" theme. The guilty party leaves for work and the Salvation Army truck parks in the driveway.

There's the story of one particular woman who got fed up with her husband's stockpiling habits. Their basement and garage looked like a thrift store exploded. You name it, they had it; piles of magazines dating back years, broken luggage, outdated TVs, ancient audio equipment, empty computer boxes. Driven to take extreme measures, she spent several hundred dollars to rent a commercial dumpster. It took the two of them an entire weekend to fill it up with a decade's worth of useless, busted, and forgettable items that should have been discarded long ago. By the way, it's been two years, but she still hasn't tossed out the business card of the carting company—just in case. Old habits die hard.

Plenty of us could take her lead. It's more than just the unsightly mess that gets to us. Clutter and disorganization first nag at us, then overwhelm us. It makes us frustrated and irritable. It eats away at our time and our sense of control. It also affects our health in ways you might not have considered.

It wasn't always like this. There's no question that we're accumulating things at a greater rate than ever before. Just visit an older home, built in the 1920s or 1930s, and you'll see that closets are narrower and fewer.

"Where did they put all their stuff?" you'll wonder. Well, they just didn't have so much of it. We live in a time of excess, graduating from bigger to better to best, and hold on to stuff from all the stages in between.

There's a saying that work expands to fill the time you have to finish the task. That holds true for storage, too. The more space you have, the more things you'll find or buy to fill it up, if you're not careful. People who move from apartments to homes wonder how they'll ever be able to fill all those drawers, closets, and pantries. Check with them a year later, and no doubt you'll find their closets bursting.

So how can you get started? What are the golden rules of organizing? Well, here they are, in no particular order:

1. Know yourself. Before organizing, identify psychological blocks, problems with your technique, and your organizational goals. This knowledge will help you toward long-term success.

2. Be flexible. Different phases of life—a new marriage, a new child, divorce, or a death in the family—present organizational challenges. Modify your systems and give yourself time to integrate these changes.

3. Be kind to yourself. In most cases, organizational challenges have nothing to do with laziness or incompetence. Other root causes are at the heart of your struggle. This book will help you to identify them.

4. Be gentle with others. As you become organizationally zealous, your family might irritate you. Work toward reasonable compromises.

5. Enlist the crew. Don't purge others' belongings when they're not around. Instead, develop systems that work for everyone.

6. Banish perfection. Your home is occupied by living beings with mess-making capacities. Home organization, especially for those with little ones, is always a work in progress.

7. Watch your wallet. Before you max out your credit cards, develop a plan.

8. Combat clutter. Keep excess out of your home. When you acquire something new, let go of something old. Only keep items that are beautiful, are useful, or have significant emotional value.

9. Make it fun. As you organize, pipe in music or a radio program you love, and be sure to reward yourself for each success along the way.

10. Love your home. Even if you don't live in the home of your dreams, relish the elements of your dwelling that bring you joy.

Not sure how to put these rules into practice? Don't worry about it. We're here to help. You're ready to tackle the clutter zones in your home, so congratulations! You've made a great start. *Simply Organized* offers you real-world strategies for getting your home back under your control, one room at a time. You'll find space you didn't know existed, even in the smallest of apartments. No need to be a professional contractor or pony up the big bucks to hire one. Each chapter gives you easy-to-implement ideas, many of which won't cost you anything more than your time and some sweat equity.

Getting organized is also a matter of getting into good habits. Let's face it. Sometimes it's just easier to pile the laundry on the guest bed "for the time being" instead of putting it away in its proper place, or to jam the golf equipment into the already overstuffed closet instead of dedicating a proper space to it. *Simply Organized* equips you with a game plan to manage it all. Plus, you'll get insider information on great products on the market that can change your lifestyle and transform your outlook.

When you streamline your living space, the ripple effects are astounding. Relationships improve, productivity soars, and serenity reigns.

Let's get started.

part 1

getting it together

IF YOU'VE PICKED UP THIS BOOK, you're probably itching to get organized. Maybe your house is in pretty good shape, but the garage and attic are completely out of control. Or perhaps your home is so chaotic that you have to dig a trail through the clutter to get from your front door to your kitchen. Whatever your situation is, this book can help you as you take small, concrete steps toward your goals.

These first few chapters will help get you started, help you figure out why you have so much difficulty being organized in the first place, and teach you how your new organized lifestyle can even help you earn some money.

Chapter 1

Control Your Clutter

WANT TO LIVE A CLUTTER-FREE LIFE? Who doesn't? But it's tough when we all seem to be battling a case of affluenza—too much affluence, which usually translates into too many things. If one of something is good, two must be better, right? Look around and you'll realize how counterproductive that thinking really is.

In fact, the first step in organizing your home is to purge. Too much clutter will make the task overwhelming and oppressive. Once you've managed to clear out a bit of the excess, you'll be better able to prioritize and to feel that you are capable of tackling the tasks at hand.

In this chapter, you'll learn the basics of culling, sorting, and organizing, and you'll explore the pleasures of clutter-free living. This chapter will also explore the emotional dimensions of clutter—the interpersonal struggles surrounding it, as well as the fresh possibilities that a streamlined home creates to help you.

Living in the Material World

Death and taxes may be inevitable, and plenty of people would add some degree of clutter to the list. There's a reason that there's a national Clutter Awareness Week (the third week in March, by the way). Even neat and tidy types have hot spots in their homes, places that seem to attract a mess. No doubt you have a few, too. Perhaps it's by the front door, where you put your keys and dump the newspaper and mail. Or is it in the kitchen, the whirlwind spot of family activities? How about the master bedroom? It's one of the last places guests see, making it an easy place to let things go.

The Bottom Line

Need proof that we're busting out of our homes? The self-storage industry is a $15 billion business. There are nearly 50,000 self-storage facilities nationwide. The Self Storage Association, the trade organization and official voice of its global membership, celebrated its thirtieth anniversary in 2005.

It's not just you. Homes all over America are brimming with clutter. And there are plenty of red flags when your clutter is getting out of control: Closets are stuffed to capacity, triggering a small avalanche each time one is opened, every flat surface is piled with paper, and the basement and attic are filled with unidentifiable items. Your mail is often mislaid. You have to scavenger-hunt through closets for something to wear. You notice in August that your Christmas lights are still hanging on the windows. It can be hard to realize that nothing in your house has a dedicated home of its own. What often starts out as a messy drawer or two turns into a carton or two full of junk. Then, before you know it, you're renting a self-storage unit in town to house your overflows. This kind of situation can obscure even the most beautiful homes.

Ideally, a home is an oasis of peace, rest, and comfort in the midst of a chaotic world. But keeping out the chaos is no small undertaking. The mailbox brims with junk mail and catalogs, and products in every mall cry out, "Take me home!" Each holiday brings a fresh deluge from well-meaning friends and family.

When clutter begins to take over, it can become almost impossible to find solace in a home. Instead of feeling a wave of peace rush over you when you pass through the door, you might instead feel a sense of dread, duty, or guilt. You might hope to get to it all one day, but the task only seems to grow more daunting with time. The temptation is to just put it off indefinitely. You might say to yourself, "I'll try to do that tomorrow, or when the kids are back in school . . . or maybe when they head off to college."

This temptation, while it might be enticing, is really only a means of prolonging the agony. And it is draining to live in a home that continually drags you down, demanding more from you than you are able to give it.

Word to the Wise

How does clutter makes you feel? Try to be aware of your emotional response to overstuffed closets and chaotic drawers. Do you feel helpless, depressed, or angry? Realize that although those emotions are part of life, you do have the power to begin to take small steps toward transforming your environment, as well as the emotions that environment evokes.

Clutter steals space from the more precious things in life, complicating daily rituals and intensifying already stressful situations. Have you ever tried to track down a lone shoe in an abyss of a closet for a pre-schooler who is already late for school? Ever been tardy to a meeting because you were searching for an important document in mountains of paper? Ever miss a credit card payment because the bill got caught in a stack of unread newspapers? When the home is cluttered, simple things in life become complicated. Life can feel as frenzied and chaotic as our homes. Clutter consumes time, energy, and psychic space that could be spent enjoying your children, cooking a nice meal, or sipping coffee on the window seat and watching the world go by.

When clutter suffocates, it not only steals time, it saps energy. If you find that you are consistently exhausted in your own home, it might be clutter that is dragging you down. There is a physical component to this emotional experience—piles of paper, books, and clothing attract dust mites and other allergens. Not only does it feel harder to breathe in a cluttered home, it is harder to breathe!

The Bottom Line

According to the principles of feng shui, cluttered corners trap precious energy and restrict the flow of life through homes. Ideally, clutter will be purged out of your home so that energy can move freely through the home. This practice could result in a much more restful home environment for you and your family.

Clutter's Causes

So how did we get here? The core issue is overconsumption. Barry Izsak, president of the National Organization of Professional Organizers, says consumers are being bombarded with messages from the media, and the message is: Get more stuff. Americans have more disposable income than ever, so it's easy to heed the messages. We're acquiring stuff without thinking what we're going to do with it, how we're going to use it, or where we're going to put it.

And, frankly, who's got the time to figure it out? We're busier than ever. Chalk it up to work, family, school, hobbies, or usually, all of the above. Our complicated lives are catching up to us. Add to that the recent trend toward nesting, spending more time indoors, embarking on more household projects, and doing more in-home entertaining, and you've got lots of good excuses to let things spiral out of control.

Word to the Wise

Ready to purge, but want someone else to handle the heavy lifting? A company called 1-800-GOT-JUNK (*www.1800gotjunk.com*) took the idea of the old TV show *Sanford and Son* and professionalized it. It's the first branded, full-service junk removal service. Two people will show up at your door and cart away just about anything they can lift—as long as it's not hazardous.

In some instances, though, it's not a matter of schedule overload. It's a matter of stopping to consider where we are in our lives and if the trappings that surround us still fit, still make sense. Now that the kids are grown and out of the house, do you really need all those extra place settings, towels, and linens? If golf is your sport of choice, can't you get rid of the in-line skates, step exercise videos, and tennis rackets in your basement? Storage spaces are often needlessly junked up because we don't stop to reevaluate our changing lives. There are emotional reasons for hoarding too. Read on!

Hoarding for Practical Reasons

There are many people who've been trained at the waste-not-want-not school of housekeeping. They've lived through the Depression years, or at least some very lean times, and they wouldn't consider throwing something out. The thinking goes that if it still functions, it stays. After all, you never know when you might need it. That perfectly good alarm clock is impossible to part with even though there are clocks on your VCR, cable box, microwave oven, and computer. These tend to be the same people who amass accidental collections. You know, like the plastic containers from Chinese take-out, plastic cutlery from fast-food restaurants, and the glass vases from too many floral deliveries to count. Trashing these things somehow seems extravagant, so they go on shelves or in drawers, where they stay put. And it seems many couples have passed this mindset onto their children.

The Childhood Roots of Adult Clutter

The tendency to hoard objects is often passed from one generation to the next. Clutter is never just about "stuff." Your possessions represent essential links to other people, and to ideas you have about yourself. Most people are pretty oblivious about the messages they unconsciously received as children that continue to influence their actions today.

Watch Out!

Clutter can have a negative effect on your social life, especially if the fear of letting others see your home keeps you from entertaining. As you begin to bring order to your home, your confidence will grow and you might be able to widen your circle of friends as well.

For those who experienced trauma as children—such as the death of a parent, a divorce, or extreme poverty—material possessions may be loaded with far more meaning than their mere physical value. A person might be tempted to hold on to items they no longer need because at some point in their lives, they lost something (or someone) they deeply valued. The pain of this loss may cause them to think that the only way they can protect themselves from more loss is to accumulate things. The stuff they accumulate becomes an armor of sorts, creating a kind of insulation from the ravages of the outside world, but also keeping a person trapped inside.

Divorce

In the book Between *Two Worlds: The Inner Lives of Children of Divorce*, Elizabeth Marquardt interviews numerous adult children of divorce to see how their childhood experiences impact their lives today. One of the chapters is entirely devoted to questions surrounding "stuff." For many adult children of divorce, the experience of having their parents separate meant more than a change in family structure. It may have caused a move from a large house to a two-bedroom apartment. It may have meant that quickly, without warning and under extreme pressure, these children had to give up multiple items that they treasured. This kind of experience can cause a person to believe that no matter how much stuff they have, they need to hold on to it all, because they never know what change is around the bend.

Word to the Wise

If you find yourself holding on to items long after they've outlived their use (for purely emotional reasons), consider taking a photo of the object to be stored in your digital files. That way, you retain a record of the person or experience associated with the object, without retaining the burden of the object itself.

Just as trauma can sometimes be passed from one generation to the next—as can tendencies toward alcoholism, emotional or physical abuse, or mental illness—the tendency to hoard material objects can easily pass from one generation to the next. If your parents (unconsciously) taught you that hoarding was necessary, they may have also conveyed to you that no matter how many possessions you owned, you would never have enough. These kinds of messages can be a huge stumbling block to a person who hopes to live in an orderly, serene, and uncluttered environment.

The Need for Abundance

The first step on the path to overcoming these messages is to learn what they are. So often, people, especially children, receive messages uncritically. From your adult perspective, try to think about what your parents conveyed to you through their relationship with stuff. If they had a deprivation mentality, you might also feel a great need for abundance.

An Organized Inquiry

Does having clutter around make it more difficult for me to clean my house? Yes! Professional cleaners estimate that by eliminating clutter, cleaning time can be reduced by as much as 40 percent.

In Julie Morgenstern's book *Organizing from the Inside Out*, she writes about a deep-seated need that many people have for abundance. It is her theory that these are the people who consistently buy in bulk and struggle to let go of things even when they are no longer useful. Morgenstern does not believe that pack rats must become purgers. Instead, she feels that it is most ideal to work with a person's need for abundance instead of trying to thwart it. In contrast to most philosophies of home organizing, she does not demand that her clients immediately purge. Instead, she tries to help them bring order to their environment, and expects that as the order improves, people become more discerning about their possessions.

In contemporary consumer culture, it is often far easier to acquire things than it is to purge them. If your parents hoarded multiple useless items because they "might need them someday," you might have inherited a similar attitude toward possessions. To be fair, there are many purgers out there who do manage to get rid of possessions they still need and may be forced to go out to the store to replace items that they once owned. Blind zeal can be as dangerous for the purger as it is for the pack rat.

Still, it is often easier to replace certain items when necessary than it is to manage multiple unused items in your home. Keep this in mind if you want a clean, orderly home—clutter resists clean. The first critical battle for the home organizer is the war on clutter. If you can begin to develop a strategic approach to clutter, you'll be in a much better position to bring order to your home.

While people may disagree about how streamlined a home needs to be, it is clear that finding ways to simplify your life does help with organization. As Victoria Moran wrote in her book *Shelter for the Spirit*, "Be forewarned: If you organize before you simplify, things will be disorganized again in no time. This is not because you're a hopeless slob without a prayer for redemption. It is because excess cannot be organized. If it could, it would not be excess."

Professional Help

At the extreme end of the clutter spectrum are folks who suffer from what some call disposophobia—fear of disposing. In other words, they hoard. According to one report, nearly a million junkaholics suffer from this psychological disorder, and the proof is in the piles. To help those who suffer from disposophobia, a national support group called Clutterers Anonymous models itself after the twelve-step format of Alcoholics Anonymous. They hold meetings in towns across the country. Some experts believe clutter in the extreme may be tied to obsessive-compulsive disorder, attention deficient disorder, or depression. Believe it or not, control freaks can be the messiest. They concentrate on trying to control everything around them, and since they're unable to keep up with their own messiness, they believe they're in control as long as no one is allowed to throw their things out.

An Organized Inquiry

How can I tell if someone is a compulsive clutterer?

According to the group Clutterers Anonymous, there are twenty warning signs, including these:

- You miss deadlines because you can't find the paperwork to finish the project.

- Your clutter is starting to affect your personal relationships.

- You bring items into the home without a place for them.

- You have difficulty disposing of things, even though you haven't used them in years.

- You possess more things than you can comfortably handle.

Most people, however, just need a little help strategizing their living space and optimizing their storage capabilities. The fact is that previous generations simply didn't have all the stuff we have today. They never had to contend with overflowing closets and burgeoning basements, even the annoying mailboxes full of junk mail. Generations from baby boomers to millennials may have it all within reach, but most haven't learned how to keep it in balance. Our homes continue to grow fuller, even as our households grow smaller. It's easy to internalize and say that a cluttered home is the result of a personality flaw, but in most cases it's simply the case of never having learned the right organizational skills.

Organized Grime

If you're embarrassed to invite company over and cringe at the thought of an unexpected drop-in by a neighbor, you're ready for a change. Sometimes it takes seeing your home through someone else's eyes to get a reality check. The look in a visitor's eyes can say it all. There's the story of one woman whose situation came home to roost in the most ironic way. Fed up with the chaos, she remembered a home organization book she had bought years earlier. Trouble was, she couldn't find it under the mess!

Living in clutter is more than just a matter of aesthetics. Clutter is an energy-sapper that takes its emotional toll and steals domestic joy. If home is where the heap is, you'll be more stressed, less productive, and pretty grumpy, too. Suddenly things start feeling out of control. "Where's the remote?" "This aspirin is expired." "I can't find my argyle socks!" Sound familiar? And it can get even worse. Clutter can cause tension and lead to disagreements in relationships, even with friends and business associates. People are chronically behind schedule because they can't find their car keys or they're unable to sift through their closets for a complete outfit in the morning. And children can suffer as well. Some youngsters experience problems at school because they're routinely late for class or underprepared for assignments. Home, a place that's supposed to be a haven, turns into one of high anxiety. And trying to avoid the issue actually adds more stress to your life. It's a vicious cycle of self-deprecation. Is it any wonder why more and more people are retreating to day spas to get a little rest and relaxation?

Watch Out!

There's such a thing as visual clutter, too. When you have a room with too many disparate objects on the walls—shelves, pictures, bulletin boards, decorative plates—it can create a crowded, overwhelming effect. That's especially counterproductive in bedrooms, the place people typically want to be a room of refuge and serenity. Try to strike a design balance.

There are plenty of times when closet and cabinet doors seem like a godsend. They make it easy to keep clutter out of sight. On the other hand, they can be a crutch that enables us to continue bad habits.

Envision what your space would look like neat and streamlined. How would you feel? More relaxed? In a better state of mind? Would you be proud to invite people over? The benefits of putting a storage and organization plan into play are transforming. You feel cleansed, calm, and accomplished. You may think you've reached the point of no return, but in fact, big returns are coming your way by investing time and employing a few simple strategies. You can do it!

Chapter 2
Start Small

THE CHINESE PHILOSOPHER LAO TZU WROTE, "A journey of a thousand miles begins with a single step." This is true for interior journeys as well as the larger external ones. This chapter offers a sampling of "baby steps" to help you on the journey. This is not about achieving perfection; rather, it is about learning to walk, to take small, concrete steps toward realistic goals that can make your home more serene, inviting, and orderly.

Check Your Expectations

One of the biggest temptations in almost every area of life is the impulse to try to take on too much, too fast. This is a huge problem when it comes to homes. Instead of trying to tackle organizational problems in small, manageable steps, people are often tempted to try to take on the whole project at once—to plan a kitchen remodel while organizing the bathroom, sweeping the garage, and vacuuming the living room.

When too much is taken on too fast, people quickly experience "crash and burn" syndrome. One can quickly become discouraged, paralyzed, and exhausted, collapsing on the sofa and looking around with despair. But it doesn't have to be this way!

Watch Out!

According to Julie Morgenstern, many people put off organizing simply because they imagine that the task will be too time consuming. Try to generate a realistic estimation of the time that each project might take you, and schedule your projects accordingly.

Let's face it. It took weeks, months, maybe even years of neglect for your home to reach the state it's in, so it's only fair it'll require a little bit of time—and elbow grease—to undo the damage. By keeping your expectations in check—and generating only small, manageable goals, such as to spend five minutes a day sorting the bedroom closet—you are more likely to keep going, even when you feel tired. After all, small, achievable goals don't weigh on you as heavily as larger ones can. You know that your goal is realistic when it feels doable. A sense of despair is a good sign that your goals are too lofty and that they need to be cut back down to size.

Overcoming Resistance

Stephen Pressfield's book *The War of Art* defines "Resistance" as the universal derailing force that seeks to undo us the moment we attempt to move to a higher plane in art, academics, relationships, and life. If Resistance had a voice, it would say things like, "You can't, you can't, you can't. You're not smart enough, organized enough, savvy enough."

If you are attempting to bring order to your home, you can expect to experience some Resistance. It can come from the inside or from the outside. You might doubt yourself, and others might question your motives, especially if they are losing the war against Resistance in their own lives. Remember—it is far easier for other people to point out the flaws in your plan than it is for them to wage their own battles.

According to Pressfield, when you feel overly critical of other people, that is a good sign that you need to stop focusing on others and channel your energies into waging your own battles. Perhaps home organizing seems too menial for these battles to be fierce. But the battles you wage on the home front are every bit as real and significant as the ones that are waged out there in the "real world." In fact, because a home is so closely linked to a sense of well-being and peace of mind, the steps you take at home can, to some extent, predetermine your success (or lack of it) in the outside world.

The Problem with Perfectionism

Perfectionism can paralyze. As soon as you realize all there is to do and all that you hope to accomplish, you can quickly become overwhelmed. Instead of trying to do everything, Pressfield recommends that you just seek to combat Resistance for a little bit every day. He recommends taking small, concrete steps that are not focused on outcomes. Instead of seeking to tackle all of your projects, he advises, just fight Resistance a little bit each day. Even if you can't make your home perfect, you can certainly make it better.

One Life or Two?

"Most of us have two lives," writes Pressfield. "The life you live, and the unlived life within us. Between the two stands Resistance." It could also be said that most people have two homes—the home you dream of living in and the home you actually inhabit. Although economics and other factors may keep you from purchasing your "dream home," it might be possible, in small, concrete ways, to bridge some of the gaps between dreams and reality just by organizing and ordering the home you actually do have, right now. If you can bring order and serenity to your home, your contentment will increase. You might even discover that you don't actually *need* all the things you imagine you do. Just do the best you can with what you have in the present moment, recognizing that your resources (time, money, energy) are finite, but if you keep taking baby steps, your possibilities will expand.

Clutter-Busting

Getting organized is a little like dieting. There are a lot of ways to accomplish the goal, and some systems work better for some than others. Ellen keeps herself on the straight and narrow by hiring a weekly cleaning service. It forces her to tidy up, clear off the tabletops, and scoop up the piles on the floor on a regular basis so that the cleaning service can actually get in there to dust and vacuum. Then there's Mindy, who always thought she had to de-clutter her whole house all at once. She says she didn't sign onto the "one area at a time" approach until she was so overwhelmed that it was the only way possible to handle her situation. And it worked.

Word to the Wise

Organization has to be based on the personality, environment, habits, and usage of the individual or household. A one-size-fits-all solution won't work. Trying to force-fit answers may work for a while, but sooner or later, anything forced is doomed to fail. Make sure your clutter-busting solutions fit your lifestyle.

There are, however, some basic habits everyone can adopt that will make a big difference. Think in terms of economy of motion and time. Take off your coat and hang it up in one fell swoop. Undress near your closet so that you automatically hang up your pants instead of tossing them on the bed. When you open your mail, read it and decide if it should be torn and trashed or filed right then and there. And then do it. Keep trash containers handy so there's no excuse to let unwanted things lie around. Sure, you have to allow for life's realities, but a good rule of thumb is to deal with something once. And remind yourself to take an inventory of your changing needs from time to time. Dispose of the items that no longer fit your lifestyle.

Find A Place for Everything

Another important ground rule? Never buy anything unless you have a place to put it. One newly purchased painting was designated for duty in the communal storage bin of a condo complex after the homeowner was unable to find the wall space on which to hang it. Another individual bought a mahogany antique icebox thinking she could convert it into a funky bar for her den. Turns out the icebox didn't fit in the den. But it does fit in her unfinished basement, where's it been collecting dust ever since. And that goes for storage containers, too. Ariane Benefit says disorganized people tend to have more organizing products than their shipshape counterparts. The containers actually add to the clutter problem because they were purchased without a specific purpose in mind. Plan first, buy second.

What works? What doesn't? Every item needs a home, and the home must suit the need. For instance, things you use every day should be stored in accessible and intuitive places. Toothpaste in the medicine cabinet is a no-brainer. But what about your house keys? Is searching for them part of your morning out-the-door routine? That's because you haven't designated a permanent and appropriate spot for them, which, in this case, would be on a hook or in a drawer right by the door. Similarly, there are times when people see an open space in a drawer or cabinet and find it impossible to resist filling it with items that don't belong. They'll put photographs in a night-table drawer or toys in a home office closet. That only starts the snowball effect of creating a storage nightmare. Take a look around your rooms, and you'll discover this is where many clutter problems originate.

Make Cleaning a Family Affair

Take a holistic approach to organizing your home. Involve each family member in the planning and process. Make sure everyone knows the end goal and what is expected of him or her. Start with a needs assessment. Who does what in which room? Do you need to carve out a crafts area? A play zone? A quiet zone for homework? A makeshift home office? How will the rooms have to be rejiggered to support these various activities? Put a budget together for shelves, bins, and other storage supplies. Then, get everyone's input and buy-in to the plan. When family members understand how integral they are to the endeavor and the benefits they'll reap, you'll have taken a major step at the outset to reaching your goals.

Try the Five-Minute Pickup

The FlyLady, Marla Cilley (*www.flylady.net*), the founder of the SHE (Sidetracked Home Executive) organizational method, offers this simple directive. Instead of trying to tackle all household chores in one fell swoop, try a five-minute pickup. This means that you set a timer for five minutes, or another short, realistic time span, and then rush around the house picking up things as quickly as you possibly can. This technique is fun and fast and will help alleviate some of the drudgery of cleaning and organizing.

The Bottom Line

A variation on the five-minute pickup game is to play it with your children and let them each have a bag or basket. You set the timer and they race around the house collecting as many items that need to be put away as they can. When the timer goes off, whoever has the most items "wins." Then the timer is set again and everyone scrambles to get everything in their baskets put away before the next ding.

It can become a race against the clock as you seek to restore order in a minimal amount of time. It can also help curb the perfectionism that so often haunts household projects, because you just can't afford to demand perfection from yourself when you're trying to beat the clock. The other great benefit of a quick pickup is that it can show you how simple it can be to tidy up. Finally, this method frees us from one of the great temptations that can sabotage our efforts—nostalgia.

Keep Moving

Often, when you begin to tackle a pile of paper you come across things that you want to study and read—old letters, old photos, and ancient report cards. While these items can be fun to peruse, you need to remember that during the five-minute pickup, nostalgia is your enemy. It will slow you down and prevent you from being objective about clutter.

An Organized Inquiry

How can I keep myself from sifting through all those nostalgic items I find? If decluttering puts you in a nostalgic mood and you want to pick up the pace instead of reading all those old letters and cards, create a box for items to go through before bed or over coffee in the morning. Promise yourself that you'll eventually give these items the time they deserve, but for now you'll simply focus on organizing.

As you go through your possessions, make sure that you remain focused on your goals. Professional housekeepers are able to make a living because they are not emotionally invested in the items they clean. They don't stop to write back to a long-lost friend in the middle of the workday or to peruse old photo albums. Because they know that the clock is ticking, they don't waste time. If you only allow yourself to work for a predetermined amount of time, you might be better able to focus on the work at hand and to accomplish your goals.

Be Positive

Another way to increase the fun of this activity is to introduce some kind of reward. You might consider putting a pot of coffee on to brew. As the aromatic coffee sputters in the pot, you rush around trying to create order. You promise yourself that as soon as the coffee is ready, you can sit and relax with a steaming cup of coffee in your orderly home.

Word to the Wise

Julie Morgenstern recommends using before and after photos as a way to celebrate a job well done. These photos will help you to remember how far you've come and what is possible if you just devote some time and energy to each room in your home.

Eventually, you might find that order has it own rewards, but when you're trying to develop positive habits, it can be helpful to attach rewards to the tasks you dread, so that instead of thinking "No pain, no gain," you will be more inclined to think of your tasks in a positive way.

Fill 'er Up

There are hundreds of products and services available to help you meet whatever specific storage challenges you're about to face. Almost any piece of furniture can be designed for functionality. There are ottomans with beneath-the-seat storage, pop-up television sets that won't commandeer surface space, and double-duty armoires. Products range from inexpensive Rubbermaid bins to top-of-the-line custom-built solutions with stratospheric price tags to match. Budget limitations are no excuse to keep the status quo. Even if you're on austerity, you can repurpose existing furniture and organizational aids in ways that don't break the bank.

The least expensive way to get more storage space, of course, is to donate, sell, or throw out. According to one report, 80 percent of what we have we never use.

The Bottom Line

The week between Christmas and New Year's Day is the biggest selling period for storage containers. The reason? Consumers need them to store their holiday decorations and to hold all their newly received gifts. Other peak selling times are back-to-school season and Halloween. Chances are you'll be able to find some good storage bargains if you time your purchases just right.

You can find storage products at hardware stores, storage specialty retailers, even museum shops. Visit the storage section of your local department store, and you'll get a good idea of just how widespread a problem clutter is these days. The aisles are packed. It's like going to a supermarket the day before Thanksgiving.

The biggest thing you'll have to cough up is not money but time. Finding long-term storage solutions is not a matter of neatening up the piles on your office desk. It's a commitment to eviscerating them. It's not hanging the clothes that sit on the foot of your bed. It's going through every scarf, pair of pants, shirt, and hat and committing to a take-no-prisoners approach.

As you go along, you'll discover a mountain of items you no longer need. Sell them. (We'll discuss this in more detail in Chapter 3.) Have a garage sale, list them online with eBay, bring them to a consignment shop, or take out a classified ad in your local paper. It's a great way to free up space and put money in your pocket. And, if you're like most people, you'll also discover items you forgot you even had, like a brand-new shirt stuffed in the back of the bedroom closet. Then again, nothing makes you feel quite as good as donating your unwanted items to a good cause.

Watch Out!

When buying storage products that require assembly, be sure to check the label for information on installation hardware. Sometimes the hardware is included with the product. Other times, you'll need to purchase it separately. Also ask the sales representative how difficult the product is to assemble. If you're an all-thumbs type, you may need to make arrangements for professional installation.

You may come up with another discovery—that you might not be storage-deprived after all. A whole-house purge can result in big chunks of newfound space. Imagine finding an extra 25 or 50 percent more space you didn't realize you had. If that doesn't motivate you, nothing will.

Save the Date

So now that you've got a plan, it's time to set a date. Grab a calendar and create a schedule. If you want to get your kitchen in primo shape for a party, allow enough time to turn it inside out and upside down. Factor in the configuration of your home and the climate, too. If you live in the north, bedrooms, kitchen, and bathrooms make good projects for the winter months. Shift your schedule if you live in a hot and humid environment.

But no matter how you decide to go about your organization project, remember to take it one step at a time. And if you need an extra incentive, keep in mind that good organization reduces stress and saves time. When you know exactly where your things are, you put an end to hide-and-seek expeditions. And many people say the process is a cathartic one that will reward you with a sense of accomplishment, self-confidence, and empowerment. And guess what! It may even earn you some money? Want to learn how? Read on!

Chapter 3
Sell Your Stuff

YOU MAY BE SURPRISED TO LEARN that clutter drains your pocketbook as well as your spirit. Those who live in overstuffed homes are more likely to lose important paperwork, such as credit card bills and checks. When there is too much clutter and important items disappear, you might be forced to run to the store for something you already own. This chapter explores the hidden cost of clutter and some ways to sell your way out of it.

Time Is Money

While you may think that the clutter in your home costs nothing to keep, most people do lose money on clutter. Having too many possessions may keep you from being able to find the things that you need when you need them, and sometimes when items can't be found quickly, you might be tempted to rush to the store to replace the item.

Not only does clutter affect your home life, it can also spill into your professional life. Those who lose things because of unmanaged clutter may suffer a loss in credibility as well. If you are a professional who is regularly late to meetings or misses deadlines because of misplaced proposals, notes, and the like, you can expect that your business will suffer because people will be wary of trusting you with important documents and projects.

Not only does clutter (and the resulting chaos) undermine your reputation, it can cause you to waste precious energy and time searching for things that could be kept in an easily accessible spot. This kind of chaos can also prevent you from being fully present to the work at hand. Instead of being able to focus on your current task, your mind rushes in a thousand different directions.

When you are distracted by piles of clutter and the nagging feeling that you'll never be able to get them under control, work takes longer and is generally less impressive in the end. Focus comes with an ability to see what is essential and central.

Word to the Wise

Another problem with clutter and disorganization is that it may interfere with your ability to pay bills on time. Late fees and increased APRs on credit cards can greatly increase your cost of living over the years. Not only that, but missed bills can negatively affect your credit rating. Nobody needs these kinds of marks against him— especially if the problem is not actually lack of funds, but rather lack of organization.

The other area that will cost you in terms of clutter is your home—if at any point you want to sell your home, the first thing you'll need to do is purge the clutter. Clutter can greatly detract from the ambiance and appearance of your home. Realtors generally believe that an uncluttered home will create a far more favorable impression for potential buyers—buyers need to be able to see into the farthest reaches of your closets. They also must quickly see the innate beauty of your home, which can easily be obscured by clutter. Likewise, the respect and love you devote to your home by keeping it tidy and uncluttered communicates to potential buyers that your home is worth their energy, love, and money.

Are You Sitting On a Gold Mine?

The bad news is that clutter is costly. The good news, however, is that hidden in your clutter there may be many items of value. When you dig deep into chaotic drawers and closets you might be surprised at the things you find—attractive clothes, important records, long-lost love letters. You never know what will turn up; the clutter could conceal items of both financial and emotional value.

The Bottom Line

In recent years, people have shown renewed interest in digging up old items and seeing what they're worth. From that painting that used to hang above Grandma's couch to the vase you got at a garage sale, you might find some truly valuable items tucked away in the dark corners of your home. Anything that doesn't have sentimental value that can be sold might be worth some money.

As you sort through the clutter, you'll probably find items that have been missing for some time. Perhaps you'll find that you have plenty of clothes that you like and that fit, and you won't need to replace your winter wardrobe after all. Perhaps you'll find your older child's snowsuit and boots and you can pass them on to your younger child instead of being forced to purchase something new. A few lucky souls may even find gift certificates they'd forgotten about, or valuable items such as a working scanner or fax machine that can be sold online for a decent price. While your clutter may be costly for you to keep, it may have value that you haven't yet discovered. Especially now that items are widely sold online, you can often recoup at least some of your initial investment.

Have a Yard Sale

One way to earn a bit of extra cash through getting rid of your unwanted stuff is to hold a yard sale or garage sale. Before embarking on this type of project, know what you're getting into and plan accordingly. A yard sale is an excellent opportunity to sell unwanted furniture, knickknacks, clothing, used sports equipment, jewelry, collectibles, and other personal and/or household items. Keep in mind, however, that at best, you'll probably receive only a fraction of what you originally paid for the items you're selling. People who attend yard sales do so in search of bargains. If they find something they want, they will likely negotiate for the lowest possible price.

Watch Out!

Yard sales can involve a significant investment of time. If you are in a rush to get your home in order, you may not want to divert your energy in this way, especially because most items can only be sold for a fraction of their original cost. Also, some towns require a permit to hold a yard sale. Check with your local town offices to find out if you need one.

After sorting through all of the rooms in your home, determine whether you have enough stuff to sell to make organizing, promoting, and actually holding a yard sale worthwhile. You may want to ask a few of your neighbors and friends to participate and sell some of their unwanted belongings as well.

Take Inventory

Take inventory of the items you plan to sell. Make a point to clean up items so that they're in the best possible condition. Then set prices for the items you plan to sell, knowing that the price you set will be a starting point for negotiation.

If you're selling clothing, give the items fair prices, keeping age and wear in mind as you determine their value. If you're selling collectibles, consider a price that's about half of what the book value is. For other types of items, set prices you think are fair, based on value and condition. You can always lower your prices during the actual sale.

One way to ensure that your prices are market appropriate is to attend several other yard sales in your community and see what prices other people are asking for similar things. Make sure you stick price tags on all of your items. You may also want to post signs stating that you're willing to negotiate. It's also an excellent strategy to offer a "buy two, get one free" offer on items such as books, videos, CDs, video games, and some types of collectibles (e.g., trading cards).

Promote Your Event

Advertising is critical for drawing a crowd. Send a notice to local newspapers stating the date, time, location, and types of items to be sold. Most community newspapers have a local calendar or events section in which yard sales are listed, sometimes free of charge. You can also take advantage of paid classified advertising, or in many cities you can advertise for free via craigslist (*www.craigslist.org*).

An Organized Inquiry

How do I price my items for a yard sale? People often overvalue their own possessions. A realistic price for a used item that is still in good condition would be between 10 percent and 30 percent of the original cost. If your sale lasts two days, drop prices even further on the second day so that you can move more items.

As for other forms of advertising, nothing is more important than plastering your community with signs. Several days before the event, post signs in your community—on lampposts, in store windows (with permission), on community bulletin boards, and in supermarkets. If you'll be selling special items, such as a rare coin collection or children's clothes, highlight this information on your signs. You also want to clearly display the date, time, and location of your event. If possible, create signs that are waterproof. Most hardware stores sell plastic "Yard Sale" or "Garage Sale" signs; you can use a permanent marker to write in the important details. It's also helpful to announce the reason for the sale. For example, your sign may say "Moving Sale."

Post your signs in high-traffic areas within a two-mile radius of your home. Your signs should answer these basic questions (but not necessarily in this order): who, what, where, when, and why. Remember to make the largest signs possible and make them easy to read. Make sure someone looking at your signs will learn the important facts quickly.

Word to the Wise

Don't overlook the power of the Internet to promote your event. Local chat rooms and message forums are an ideal place to share information about your upcoming yard sale. You can also use the Internet to seek out information about putting together a sale.

On the day of the sale, hang balloons in front of your home and at the end of your street (if possible) to draw the attention of customers. As you begin to display your items, think about setting up a large bin or table and offering a few items for free. Select items that you want to get rid of, but that you don't think people will pay money for. Not only is offering a few items for free a nice gesture, it also helps create a buyer-friendly atmosphere and will help reduce shoplifting.

Whenever possible, display your items on tables, bookshelves, or portable clothing racks. Try to keep the items organized and readily accessible. Don't make people dig through piles of stuff to find what they're looking for. Also, divide up your items into categories. For example, set aside separate areas for used sports equipment, kitchen items, clothing, CDs and videos, furniture, collectibles, and books.

Sell Items Online

If you have a few expensive items to sell, such as furniture or collectibles, consider selling those items online, using an online auction service such as eBay (*www.ebay.com*), Half.com (*www.half.ebay.com*), or craigslist (*www.craigslist.org*).

An online auction is just like a live auction: people bid on an object, which is sold to the highest bidder. A potential buyer participates by bidding on an item that a seller has listed. The person who has offered the highest bid at close of auction wins the right to purchase the item at that price.

An Organized Inquiry

Can I get someone to sell my items online for me? Sure! If selling your items online feels like too much of a headache, consider using a service, such as "Sell it on eBay," that will price, list, and ship your items for you. These middlemen always take a commission, but you may not actually lose money because their experience helps them to get the best price.

Make sure you list your items under the appropriate category within the online auction site. eBay, for example, offers a variety of main categories and subcategories, such as antiques and art, clothing and accessories, dolls and bears, jewelry, and so on. When preparing a listing, keep in mind that many potential buyers will be less likely to want to purchase an item from you if you have not posted a digital photo of the item. Also, be sure to have the following information available:

- **Title:** Include a brief, thoughtful title that accurately describes the item you are selling. A title that's easy to understand will make your item easier for bidders to find.

- **Description:** Describe the product in detail. The more detail you provide, the more confidence you'll inspire among the bidders.

- **Sales policies:** Select the types of payment you're willing to accept. These could include cashier's checks, money orders, cash, personal checks, credit cards, or an online payment option such as PayPal. (PayPal is an ideal option because the cash will be available almost immediately, although you will have to create a PayPal account.)

- **Shipping options:** Decide whether you or the buyer pays the shipping costs. Decide when the item will ship, either upon receipt of payment or immediately after the auction closes. You might also want to save yourself the hassle of shipping and say "pick-up only." Local websites, such as craigslist.org, are ideal for the pick-up-only option.

- **Quantity of item:** If you have more than one of the same item, and you would like to sell each one individually (in which case there may be several buyers), consider listing each product separately.

- **Starting price:** Enter the price that will be used to start the auction.

- **Length of auction:** Determine how many days the auction will last.

It's also very important to be completely honest about any flaws or damage on any items you're trying to sell. If you attempt to gloss over any problems with the item, you may get a very unhappy buyer. This buyer might then post negative feedback next to your name on eBay, and you could lose credibility. A loss of credibility will negatively affect your future sales.

Sell to Antique Stores or Consignment Shops

If you only have a few items you're interested in selling, and these items (such as antiques, jewelry, furniture, or collectibles) have significant value, consider working directly with an antique store or consignment shop to sell them. These shops may pay you a negotiated price up-front, or you may have to wait until the consignment shop sells your items before you receive your money. Either way, you can potentially earn cash for your unwanted items. Check the Yellow Pages for a list of consignment shops and/or antique dealers in your area. Assuming you know that the items you're hoping to sell are valuable, get them appraised independently so you know exactly what they're worth before negotiating a sale price.

You'll find a variety of consignment shop agreements. Some charge a straight commission (as much as 50 percent of the purchase price on items sold). Other shops charge space rental plus a commission, while still others charge a flat space-rental fee. For items that don't sell quickly, some shops require that you remove the merchandise or mark it down within a specified time. Be sure to ask what the policy is for the consignment shop you are considering. Also, make sure to get the terms in writing.

The Bottom Line

A fun way to become more educated about the values of antique items is to watch *Antiques Roadshow* on PBS. This show travels all around the country and offers Americans the opportunity to have their mysterious treasures and family heirlooms professionally appraised on TV. Check out the show's website: *www.pbs .org/wgbh/pages/roadshow*.

Donate Items to Charity

No matter what items you have to get rid of, one possibility is to donate them to a local charity. Depending on the charity, you can donate used clothing, furniture, appliances, vehicles, canned (or prepackaged) food items, old sports equipment, eyeglasses, and just about anything else that others might be able to use.

Word to the Wise

Take care that any item you donate to charity is in acceptable condition. Clothing that is stained, torn, or otherwise damaged should not be donated. Out of respect to these organizations and to the people who patronize them, only donate items that you would not be ashamed to own.

While you won't receive cash for making a donation to a charity, you can take a tax deduction if the charity you donate your stuff to is legitimate and provides you with a receipt. Here is a listing of some charities that might be interested in your castaways:

The Women's Alliance (*www.thewomensalliance.org*) is a national not-for-profit membership alliance of independent community-based groups that increase the employability of low-income women. Assistance provided to these women includes donated professional attire, career-skills training, and a range of support services from dental care to health and wellness programs.

Dress for Success (*www.dressforsuccess.org*) is a not-for-profit organization that helps low-income women transition into the work force. Each client receives one suit for her interview and a second suit when she lands a job.

The Salvation Army (*www.salvationarmy.org*) is an international movement, collecting a wide variety of items and selling them cheaply. They also provide jobs and training for those who work in their centers.

Volunteers of America (*www.voa.org*) is a national, not-for-profit, faith-based organization providing local service programs and the opportunity for individual and community involvement in about 300 communities across the country.

Goodwill Industries (*www.goodwill.org*) is one of the world's largest not-for-profit providers of employment and training services for people with disabilities and other conditions, such as welfare dependency, illiteracy, criminal history, and homelessness.

Should you have old computers or computer equipment on hand, consider donating them to a worthy charity. In Julie Morgenstern's book *Organizing from the Inside Out*, she lists several charities that will refurbish old computers and ship them overseas to needy children. These charities include:

- The National Cristina Foundation (*www.cristina.org*)

- World Computer Exchange (*www.worldcomputerexchange.org*)

- Computers for Schools (*www.pcsforschools.org*)

Keep in mind that computers are unsafe for landfills and should be disposed of properly. Don't try to sneak "techno-trash" in with your regular garbage. Check with your city's recycling department to see what kind of recycling options are available. Many cities offer a "blue bag" or pick-up service for electrical items. This will ensure that your items are recycled or disposed of properly. Even if you can't recoup your initial investment, nothing is completely wasted when you make an ecologically conscious decision.

part 2

room-by-room

IN THE CHAPTERS THAT FOLLOW, you'll learn about the specific storage challenges and opportunities in each room of the house. The problem area will determine what supplies you'll need for a clean sweep. Generally, you should have the following on hand:

- Cartons
- Markers (A label maker is even better. As your third-grade teacher stressed, neatness counts.)
- Labels
- Trash Bags
- File Folders
- Binders

Solving your storage problems entails getting to the heart of the matter: stuff. To know where to put it, you need to first determine if belongs in your home. Do you use it, need it, or love it? Be prepared to assess each item. There's no easy way around this job. It'll force you to take an inventory of what you've got and what you should do with it. Keep this in mind as you begin the process of organizing your home—room-by-room!

Chapter 4

Clear Out Your Kitchen

THE KITCHEN MAY BE THE HEART OF THE HOME, but it is also the place that naturally attracts the most clutter and chaos. The combination of such a wide variety of items that need to be stored and the high traffic can make this room especially challenging. We all have the fantasy of a dream kitchen—one of those tricked-out numbers packed with techno-wizardry appliances and clean, clear surfaces. You know that kitchen. You love that kitchen! But why is it so hard to come by? Have no fear. This chapter will explore a variety of ways to organize your kitchen, trans-forming it into a place of beauty, order, and simplicity, where you and your family will want to gather, cook, and linger.

Out in the Open

Is your kitchen the gathering spot for family meals, projects, and meet-ings? Do you have more gadgets than the local electronics store? Do you super-size your grocery shopping at a discount warehouse club? Chances are you've got kitchen creep, the pesky phenomenon that occurs when items start busting out of their designated spaces. The cabinet doors don't quite shut all the way; the freezer door needs an extra good push to cement the seal. And with kitchen creep inevitably comes the dreaded kitchen heap.

The kitchen is a very difficult place to keep clutter-free because it's filled with all the things you need for the smooth operation and functioning of your household. The more stuff you have, the more you need an adequate storage plan. The key is designing one that fits your lifestyle. What works for a single person will likely be inadequate for a couple and may fail miserably for a family.

The Bottom Line

Every year, the U.S. Postal Service holds its annual Stamp Out Hunger food drive. In 2009, letter carriers collected 73.4 million pounds of non-perishable donations that were delivered to local food banks, pantries, and shelters for the needy. It couldn't be easier to give. Once you get a card notifying you of the date, all you have to do is leave your donations outside your front door.

It's a fact that people are making more demands of their kitchen nowadays and forcing homebuilders, manufacturers, and contractors to meet the challenge. Time was when looking for a home, folks asked how good the schools were, how big the garage was, how old the oil burner was—all important matters, of course. But they didn't give much consideration to the kitchen. It was almost an afterthought. They never asked themselves, "Can this kitchen work for me?" Here's the good news. It *can* work, no matter what its size. We can't all have mega-square-foot kitchens with home-magazine centerfold allure. And we really don't need countertops the size of hockey rinks—at least not if we can slim our possessions down to size.

The best approach is to start at square one by taking an inventory of everything you've got in there and, essentially, turn your kitchen inside out. Think spring cleaning with a vengeance. You can dedicate small chunks of time to the task by carving out an hour here for, say, the pantry and an hour there for the refrigerator. Better still, bite the bullet and tackle the entire room all at once. It's more time efficient in the long run. What's more, it's smarter to take advantage of your let's-do-it attitude when the adrenaline is running high. An average-size kitchen might take three to six hours or more with an assistant—but only if that assistant helps you stay on task. Whatever you decide, the strategy is the same. Clear each of these areas out:

- Pantry
- Cabinets
- Under-the-sink area
- Refrigerator
- Drawers
- Broom closet
- Open shelves

Then turn into a drill sergeant. Inspect each item and be merciless. Any chipped, broken, or outdated items go straight to the trash. If you find yourself hemming and hawing over something, throw it out. Anything that's outlived its usefulness in your home might just find a purpose in someone else's. This strategy can be especially helpful when tackling the organization of your kitchen counters

Clutter-Free Countertops

In every area of home organization, begin with the basics. Kitchen counters often attract clutter, and this can lead to a crowded, defeated look. Go into your kitchen and assess the items on your counters. Do all of them need to be there? Are there some small appliances on your counters that you don't use daily (or use very rarely)? Consider finding a new home for these appliances—either tuck them away in a cabinet or give them to someone who will use them.

To free up counter space, use appliances (such as a microwave) that can be installed under your cabinets. Also, can you utilize a paper-towel rack that hangs on a wall or on the side of your refrigerator so that it doesn't take up countertop space?

Word to the Wise

We recommend that you strive to empty your dishwasher immediately after the cycle is complete. This way, you'll reduce sink clutter (no dirty dishes will get trapped in a "holding pattern") and, if your family members know that the dishwasher won't be full of clean dishes for hours on end, they'll be easier to train to fill it.

If you do your dishes by hand, beware of the dish rack. Not only can it be tempting to let dishes pile up there, but the moisture can create an ideal climate for mold and bacteria to grow (unwelcome creatures such as roaches love this kind of dank environment). You might want to buy a stainless steel rack or any rack that is easy to clean and attractive. If you begin with an attractive rack, you'll feel more inclined to keep it looking nice—you'll be better able to see it as well, when you keep those dishes moving!

Cabinets and Drawers

For some people, the idea of tackling those kitchen cabinets and drawers can be almost paralyzing. There is just so much to do and it can be hard to know where to start. Keep in mind that you don't have to do it all at once—in fact, you probably shouldn't even try, because you might crash and burn. Instead, take it one drawer and one cabinet at a time. If you can do one cabinet or drawer each day for a couple of weeks, you'll find that this small amount of daily effort will radically change the way your kitchen looks and feels.

One Drawer at a Time

To begin with, take a single drawer and dump out the contents. The incredible variety of items might even make you laugh—that's good! Enjoy learning about yourself and your own quirky habits as you organize.

Word to the Wise

Chances are you can ditch all those appliance manuals that clutter up your drawers. Virtually all manufacturers have toll-free customer service numbers and representatives on call to answer any questions or troubleshoot problems during business hours. In addition, you'll usually find around-the-clock help online at manufacturers' websites.

After you've emptied the contents of the drawer, arrange the items into three piles. These piles can be titled something like "Keep here," "Store in another place," and "Goodbye." As you reduce the bulk in each drawer, you'll find that it will be much easier to keep the drawer clean. Plus, it feels great to open a formerly cluttered drawer and find that you can immediately spot the items you need— the boost in efficiency and ease of use will be well worth your efforts. Just try organizing one drawer and see if it doesn't make you want to do more!

As you sort through your cabinets and drawers, think in terms of categories. Some entire categories of items might be able to go in another room—fine linens and china, for example, might find a place in your dining room. Special items for entertaining can also be located together so that you'll have quick access to them when company arrives.

After your kitchen items are divided into categories, determine whether each group needs cabinet space, drawer space, or some other type of storage. Will all of these items be kept in the kitchen, or will some items, such as your fine china, be kept in the formal dining area? Measure all of your available cabinet space and make sure that the items you plan to store there will fit. By arranging your food in an accessible and easy-to-spot way, you'll find that cooking is simpler. You'll also be far less likely to be confused about what you do and don't need come grocery day, and you'll save money as a result.

Watch Out!

Arrange your cupboards so that things used most frequently are in the easiest-to-reach places. Organize the pantry so that breakfast cereals, beverages, and other packaged foods are easy to locate. With spices, create a system that works for you—for instance, you can group spices as "baking spices," "cooking spices," and "ethnic spices."

Don't hold onto food items you're not likely to use, either. Making a pumpkin pie may have seemed like such a good idea when those cans of pumpkin mix were on sale, but now they're oversized paperweights that are simply wasting valuable pantry space. Don't overstock, no matter how tempting the price, especially on perishables. A bag of lemons is no bargain if the whole lot of them goes bad before you've had a chance to use them.

So, what's left in your cabinets? If you've done your job well, it shouldn't be much. Only the ingredients you'll actually be turning into meals before too long and the glassware, dishes, cleaning supplies, and appliances that are part of your day-to-day survival gear should remain. A no-frills approach can yield high returns.

An Orderly Fridge and Freezer

The first step in organizing your refrigerator and freezer is to empty them out and clean them. Remove all of the shelves and clean them. If you have glass or plastic shelves, try using a natural cleaner without harmful chemicals. Because the refrigerator is a contained and well-sealed space, you don't want chemicals compromising the indoor air quality—or leaving residue on your apples and blueberries.

Start on the top shelf. Decide what will be kept, and then throw away old leftovers—let go of items that you know you'll never eat. Open all containers and check what's inside. Throw out anything that's questionable or past its expiration date.

Word to the Wise

If you find that fruits and veggies often languish in your refrigerator, place them at eye level so that the moment you open the door you'll be enticed to eat or prepare them. An overstuffed refrigerator can also contribute to this problem. Clear out leftovers quickly so you can easily view and assess the contents of your fridge.

Next, inventory the items that belong in your refrigerator and decide how you'll organize them. Take full advantage of the drawers, shelves, and refrigerator door. Keep similar items together. Store small, loose items and leftovers in clear-plastic containers so you can see what's inside. And keep the following tips in mind when deciding where to place refrigerated foods:

- **Don't get egg on your face:** Never keep eggs in the refrigerator door. This will expose them to air each time the door is opened and closed. Instead, keep them in the carton on an upper shelf in the refrigerator.

- **Keep it crisp:** Crisper drawers are good for vegetables, such as peppers. These drawers typically have humidity controls designed to help prevent vegetables from losing moisture. (The drawers seal tightly, which limits oxygen intake. The more oxygen intake, the quicker a food will deteriorate and spoil.)

- **Watch your head:** Keep lettuce fresher by storing it unwashed in a heavy-duty zipper bag. Discard the outer leaves that contain excess moisture. Wrap the lettuce in a paper towel, insert it in the plastic bag, squeeze as much air out of the bag as possible, and seal the bag.

Following these quick tips will help you stay organized and ensure your dollar goes that extra mile!

Items for the Freezer

If you wish to store fresh herbs such as basil, store them in the freezer door in a plastic bag. In addition, store whole-wheat flour in the freezer. (White flour, however, can be stored at room temperature.) Freeze meats that you don't plan to use within three days. Store items in airtight containers, such as freezer bags and Tupperware. Make sure you date all items. Most frozen items, such as soups, casseroles and meat, can keep for several months in the freezer. Just be sure that oxygen doesn't get in and cause freezer burn, which will compromise flavor.

Room-Temperature Items

Though you may be tempted to put all fresh foods in the fridge, this isn't a good idea for certain foods. For example, don't store potatoes in the refrigerator. The starch breaks down quickly, which leaves the potato mushy if baked. In the same way, tomatoes and cucumbers should be stored at room temperature. If you want these items cold in a salad, chill them before serving. Bananas, avocados, and zucchini should also be kept out.

Inside and Out

When organizing your fridge, don't limit yourself to the inside. In many homes, refrigerators wind up becoming giant, messy canvases for magnet collages. Do your magnets multiply like rabbits? It might be handy to have the phone number of your favorite pizza delivery service, but you can put the refrigerator's magnetic properties to better use. Consolidate it all with a Fridgefile (*http://fridgefile.net*), a vertical filing and dry-erase message center that can hold menus, homework, or coupons. Small magnetic shelves are a good idea for spices, paper towels, or hooks for utensils and potholders. But don't go overboard. Refrigerators dominate a kitchen and can get cluttered in no time.

The Kitchen Sink and Everything Under It

Open up your under-sink cabinets and you'll probably find some extra room down there. Take advantage of the space by investing in adjustable-height shelving that slides out along rails and is specially designed to fit around awkward drain pipes.

An Organized Inquiry

How do I dispose of household cleaning products? Some of the household products stored under your sink may be toxic and fall under the classification of hazardous waste. Don't pour them down the drain or throw them in the trash. Contact the appropriate environmental agency for your area or call your town hall to find out how to dispose of chemical cleansers properly and safely.

In most homes, the cabinet under the kitchen sink is brimming with household cleaners. It's hard to resist sampling a new product when the manufacturer promises its newest glass cleaner, stainless steel polisher, lemon oil, and detergent will make your life easier. So what do we do? We fill up buckets with soaps of every conceivable kind for every different surface. But are they all necessary? Imagine how much space you could free up if just a handful of cleansers served multiple functions. There are a few multitasking products on the market. A product called Holy Cow (*www.holycowproducts.com*), for instance, can clean your walls, grout, and granite, and even your jewelry and shoe leather.

Use That Space

Check around your kitchen for opportunities to convert idle space into workable storage. What's below your lower cabinets, near the kick-toe area? Nothing? Good. Retrofitting that gap might be all you need to store those no-good-place-for-it items like recyclable newspapers and pet bowls.

Full-extension pullouts in cabinet drawers make pots, pans, and serving dishes easier to get to and offer up the ability to stack items more efficiently—and higher. Pullouts make reaching for items easier on your back, too.

You'll make the most out of limited space by keeping like items together. Store dishes with dishes, pots with pots, and serving trays with serving trays. Stack saucepans by size. The difference between neatly nestled and clumsy clutter are the lids, so install a separate rack for them. Pick up pullouts with wire shelf sides to prevent smaller items from falling out and causing drawer jams.

Swing-out shelves from a corner cabinet will help you exploit every spare inch. Even seemingly little add-ons—like a tilt-out sink tray for your sponges and steel wool pads—can make a marked improvement.

Drawer dividers, easily found at home goods stores, keep flatware in ship-shape. Steal a wedge of space in a base cabinet and use vertical dividers to organize baking sheets, muffin pans, trays, oversize serving platters, and cutting boards in size order. The setup keeps items tidy and prevents dishes from getting chipped. Speaking of cutting boards: You can look for one that has a drawer built right in to store knives, or you might choose to have a custom version built that's set right into a cabinet drawer.

The Bottom Line

Some bulky kitchen utensils are available in easy-to-store form. You can find flexible muffin pans, molds, and colanders made of silicone that flatten for easy storage and then spring back into shape.

You may want to consider building a pantry cabinet with slide-out shelves and built-in power strips expressly to hold small appliances. Then, when you need to whip something up in the blender or pop some bread in the toaster, just slide out the shelf and use the appliances right where they are. It's less cumbersome, more utilitarian, and very time efficient. Store your most-used appliances like the coffee maker and juicer on the most accessible middle shelf. Lesser used items, like the popcorn maker and blender, can go on higher and lower shelves.

Trash and Recyclables

What goes in must come out. This is especially the case with the kitchen, where you bring a huge amount of food, packaging, and other containers in, and many of these things will need to eventually be disposed of. Have you ever read Shel Silverstein's poem "Sarah Cynthia Sylvia Stout Would Not Take the Garbage Out"? This kind of stench and disarray can come if you don't have a good system for managing garbage and recyclables.

Choosing a Garbage Can

Garbage cans with lids are ideal for keeping bad smells in and pets out. Stainless steel can also be attractive and can endure for many years. If you purchase a can that uses a foot lever, you'll reduce the risk of picking up bacteria while cooking. After your garbage bag is full, seal and dispose of it as quickly as possible. If you're tossing food scraps, place these scraps within a small plastic bag that can be sealed and toss that into the larger garbage bag. This will reduce bad odors.

To maintain a clean environment, you'll also want to spray your garbage can with disinfectant spray (that also removes odor) and clean the garbage can itself on a regular basis.

Managing Recyclables

Recycling is a great way to reduce waste and to conserve resources. Most American cities now have dynamic recycling programs. Minimal effort is required on your part to make recycling work in your home.

First of all, make sure that you rinse all cans and glass bottles well. These bottles, cans, and boxes can stink and attract pests if they are left with residue on them. In most cities, you will be expected to foot-flatten food cartons and plastic bottles and jugs. You'll also be expected to separate green, brown, blue, and clear glass as well as newspapers and cereal boxes.

If you purchase a recycling sorter with at least two separate bins, this can simplify your task. Keep in mind, however, that, like trash, even well-rinsed bottles and cans will create a sticky, stinky residue in your bin. The bin will need to be washed frequently.

Ideally, you'll take your recycling out as quickly as possible. If you live in an area where you keep large color-coded bins out back at all times, you can simply store your recycling in plastic grocery bags and then carry them out each morning or evening. This is especially the case with newspapers—they tend to create a lot of clutter and can be cumbersome, if you try to take out too many at the same time. Just as you bring in a single newspaper each morning, try to take out (or place in a recycling container) a single newspaper each night. By tackling your recycling quickly, you can prevent the work and mess involved in managing a larger recycling system.

Clutter Is Contagious

Americans spend billions of dollars a year renovating their kitchens, turning them into status symbol jewels of the home. And then, poof! The sleek and streamlined super-kitchen façade is lost under a poor storage system. Clutter influences not only the kitchen but the adjoining rooms as well. With open floor plans featured in so many homes these days, a cluttered kitchen can affect an entire suite of rooms (including your dining room, which we'll discuss in the next chapter). Be careful! Clutter is contagious.

The best habit you can adopt when organizing your kitchen is to give yourself regularly scheduled reality checks. What do you use? What do you need? Is an item worth the counter space or cabinet space it demands? Keep in mind that the best clutter-buster is the ability to Just Say No.

Chapter 5

Create a Delicious Dining Room

AFTER YOU'VE HAD A CHANCE TO BRING SOME ORDER TO THE KITCHEN, you might get the urge to beautify your dining room as well. This chapter offers suggestions for making your dining area (whether it is a separate dining room or built into your kitchen) serene and hospitable. This chapter will also suggest an organized, simplified approach to entertaining.

Determining Your Needs

There are no rules about how to use your dining room. It is your space, and you need to trust your own instincts about how it can best be put to use for your family. Depending on the size and lighting, it could potentially be a great place for homework, meetings, and even a small home office. Even if you don't technically "work" from home, everyone needs a place for sorting through bills and managing paperwork. Your dining room could very well serve this function. Keep in mind, however, that you'll want to be able to conceal stacks of papers and bills so that meals can be peaceful.

As you think about how you can best use your dining space, you might want to keep the following questions in mind:

1. What will the primary use of this room be? (Casual dining with your family? Formal dining with friends, family, and/or business associates? Storage? Will this room double as a place for you to do work or your kids to do homework?)

2. How often will you use the dining area for dining? (Nightly, weekly, monthly, once a year? Only for holidays?)

3. How often will the dining area be used for activities other than dining?

4. How many people will you typically need to accommodate? While you may have all of your relatives over each year for Thanksgiving dinner, for example, during the rest of the year, will you typically only have four or six people dining in this room?

After you've assessed your needs for this space, you'll be better prepared to come up with a plan for using it. If you are going to use it for homework or a home office, consider investing in baskets, a filing cabinet, or some other system that can serve as a paper sorter. If your dining room will double as a workspace, keep in mind that it will probably attract massive amounts of paper, so you'll want to be prepared to make quick decisions about how to store (and when to recycle) your paper before it grows from stacks into mounds into mountains.

The Dining Room Table

The main piece of furniture in a dining room is, of course, the dining-room table. While it seems as if keeping this room organized would be easy, you are up against one big challenge here. Flat surfaces tend to attract clutter, and this can be especially true with a rarely used dining-room table or sideboard. If you want to make your dining room a place for entertaining and festive family meals, you're probably itching to get that clutter under control.

Be prepared for the reality that you're going to want to stash paper-work, half-finished school projects, and all manner of clutter on that lovely flat surface. This area, which often becomes a landing zone for mess, will need special attention to keep it clutter-free.

If you can keep your dining room in order, however, you'll find that it can be a place of refuge and peace, and that you might feel more excited about the idea of entertaining. You might need to make a com-mitment to yourself to do a nightly dining-room check, to remove all papers and other clutter on a regular basis before it accumulates. This small, regular effort will pay off when you find you want to use that table!

Another way to keep the paper clutter at bay is to do something that will make your table lovely—put out a bowl of fresh seasonal fruits or a nice tablecloth. When possible, bring in flowers from your garden and arrange them on your table. These items can serve as a reminder that your dining table should stay as clean and beautiful as possible. Beauty and order are closely related. When you seek to make different corners of your home beautiful, you are all the more likely to feel energized about keeping them orderly.

Storing Fine China

Perhaps your dining area has built-in storage or a stand-alone storage piece. This storage can be useful if you are intentional about items you place there. Not only can you keep fine china separate from your every-day dishes, but you can also keep part of this storage empty so that you have a place to stow papers and other items when company is coming.

If your cabinet has glass doors, your china will be pretty well protected as you show off the beauty of your pieces. If your fine china will be stored in drawers or closed cabinets, however, you'll want to take steps to properly protect these expensive and fragile items. Using quilted vinyl cases for china, for example, will help keep dust away, and at the same time will help prevent chipping and scratching.

Word to the Wise

To prevent chips and scratches while storing china in these padded vinyl cases, a separate soft-foam protector is placed in between each item. These cases can then be safely stored in a drawer or cabinet. Dinnerware storage pouches, manufactured from quilted cotton with acrylic felt inserts and zippered tops, can be purchased from Old China Patterns Limited by calling 800-663-4533 or by visiting the company's website (*www.chinapatterns.com*).

If a piece of your fine china, crystal, or formal flatware happens to break, chip, or get badly scratched, and your pattern or design has been discontinued, you can find companies that buy and sell discontinued china patterns and other formal dinnerware. Many of them are listed on the Set Your Table: Discontinued Tableware Dealers Directory website (*www.setyourtable.com*).

Orderly Entertaining

When planning a formal gathering, it pays to work through the details beforehand. For example, make sure that there's always a clear pathway between your kitchen and the dining area. If you'll be traveling back and forth between these two rooms, choose a seat at the table that's the closest to the kitchen, so you avoid disturbing others each time you leave your seat.

Entertaining can be overwhelming, but you can greatly simplify your task if you ask yourself some questions beforehand. These questions can help guide your decision-making process as you prepare for your guests. Questions to keep in mind include:

- What is the purpose of the gathering?

- Will this be a casual or formal dining experience?

- How many people will be attending?

- What will the complete menu include?

- Do I have enough seating, dishes, flatware, glasses, and serving items to accommodate all of the people attending the event?

- What is the schedule for the event—when will I serve drinks, hors d'oeuvres, each course of the meal?

- Would a buffet be preferable to a sit-down meal, given the nature of the gathering and the number of people I'm inviting?

- What is the theme of the event? Do I need special decorations?

As you think about these questions, you'll be able to plan an event that is suited to your needs. Be creative as you plan your event, and enjoy the process.

A Simple Affair

Even if you're not Martha Stewart, you can enjoy hosting people in your home, and you can put your guests at ease with the relaxed, hospitable atmosphere you provide. When the idea of entertaining fills you with dread, it's time to lower your expectations for yourself. Your own attitude toward the event will permeate the atmosphere, so you want to be as relaxed as possible. Sometimes the only way to be calm before company arrives is to cut back on ceremony and accept your own limitations. You might, for example, serve a fork-only buffet. If guests can only use one type of silverware, you are less likely to spend hours cooking and use multiple dishes.

Jazzing Up Takeout

First of all, there is no law against ordering takeout for guests— just use your own plates to make the meal feel more homey. You can also bring some fresh flowers in from the garden and use a nice tablecloth (perhaps with candles?) to make your home feel more welcoming. Think in terms of seasons as well—you can bring the natural world into your home any time of the year by decorating with the leaves, flowers, or fruits of the season or by playing with seasonal colors.

The Potluck Option

If you feel overwhelmed by the idea of hosting a crowd and feeding them a full meal, by all means, take people up on their offers to contribute food to the gathering—or even let them know up-front what you'd like them to bring. Some guests might even want to join you in the kitchen to prepare their dishes. Cooking with others can transform a task that feels like a chore into a joy. Potlucks are a bit of an adventure, because you never know exactly what your guests will come up with—this can be part of the fun, too. Just as all of your guests will bring their own presence into your home for the celebration, so too, they'll have a chance to plan and prepare their own piece of the feast. Keep in mind that potlucks can simplify your life in another way—the guests go home with their own large serving bowls to clean.

Choosing and Storing Table Linens

Before your guests come (and after they leave) you'll want to have a plan for your linens. They can add a lovely touch to the table, but storing them can be a little tricky. Here are some tips for making your linens work for you.

Measure First: Before you purchase table linen, be sure to know the exact measurements of your table. Pay attention to the shape of the table on the package—it can be easy to find the perfect table linen that won't actually fit when you get home. A formal tablecloth should hang down from the edge of the tabletop approximately eighteen inches.

Store Appropriately: Refrain from storing fine table linen in the original plastic packaging it may have been sold in. A plastic container or bag will trap moisture and bacteria, which could eventually cause discoloration. Also, don't store your table linens so tightly folded that they crease. Keeping a tightly folded tablecloth in an overcrowded drawer, for example, will damage the fabric over time.

Build Your Collection Over Time: If you're about to invest in an expensive tablecloth, begin your table-linen collection by choosing a classic white linen or classic damask tablecloth, along with a matching set of napkins. You can later expand this collection with a solid-color cloth that matches an accent color in your dinnerware pattern, for example.

Watch Out!

Linens alone will not protect your table. Purchase table pads to go beneath a tablecloth. These pads will greatly extend the life of your table and decrease your own panic when a hot item is set down on the table or a glass of wine spills.

Don't be afraid to wash real-linen tablecloths and napkins in your washing machine. Just set the washer to delicate and use cool water. Fine linen improves in appearance and feel with every wash. Just as you would with expensive bed linen, iron your table linen while it's still damp, on the back side. This will help prevent any shiny patches from forming. Make sure the iron isn't too hot. When storing fine table linens, always launder and iron (or professionally clean) them properly before putting them into storage.

Care for Your Flatware

When washing your fine flatware, use only warm, sudsy water. Carefully rinse away traces of food from the flatware. Avoid using harsh dishwashing detergents that contain chlorides. Also, avoid lemon-scented detergents, which contain acids that may harm the metal. It's also important to hand-dry silver, especially knife blades, to avoid spotting and pitting.

If you'll be washing both silver and stainless-steel flatware in the dishwasher, don't put them in the same basket section. You want to avoid allowing one metal to touch the other.

While sterling silver is beautiful, it tarnishes over time and keeping your flatware shining is one aspect of the "glory work" involved in making your dining space work. There are many different metal polishes on the market. Some polishes can be corrosive, so take care to follow the manufacturer's instructions. While polishing can be a headache, it can also be satisfying because the results are almost immediate—polishing your flatware can make it feel as though you're getting a whole new set for just the cost of the polish.

Watch Your Wine

Whether you have a stand-alone liquor cabinet or a wine rack built into your buffet or credenza, keep all of your related supplies together in one area. In addition to the actual bottles of wine and liquor, some of the supplies you'll want on hand in or near your liquor cabinet include a bottle opener, bottle stoppers, cocktail napkins, cocktail shaker, corkscrew, decanter, foil cutter, ice bucket, pitcher, wine glasses, shot glasses, and a bartender's mixing guide. Some wine racks have special shelves or cabinets to store these accessories.

By paying special attention to how you arrange and keep your dining space, you can create a room that has ambiance, charm, and order. The more care you put into making your dining room lovely, the more joy you will find in the meals you share there with your family and friends. This joy can extend to other areas of your life—and home—as well. As Virginia Woolf said, "One cannot think well, love well, sleep well, if one has not dined well."

Chapter 6

Love Your Living Room

THE LIVING ROOM TENDS TO BE A HUB OF ACTIVITY IN ANY HOME—people gather there to watch television or study, children play there, guests are entertained there. As a result, many living areas become centers of clutter and confusion. This chapter will explore a few methods for making your living space orderly, inviting, and serene.

The Plan for Your Living Room

Because this room is a meeting place where everyone in the house goes, it can often get bogged down with "stuff." Julie Morgenstern reduces the problem to a very basic root—so much goes on in the living room, yet many people do not assign "homes" to the clutter. If, for example, your children play in that room but all of their toys are still relegated to their bedrooms (with the expectation that they—or you—will carry these items to their room every night), it might be wiser to put a toy basket in the living room so that putting toys away will be less of a challenge. If you like to read in this room but the books, newspapers, and magazines tend to pile up on the coffee table, you could think in terms of a few baskets—one for paper products that are ready for the recycling bin and another for those publications that you're still reading.

Before going out and investing in all-new living-room furniture, try rearranging the furniture you have now and accenting or accessorizing to create a whole new look in the room. Simply by rearranging the furniture into a more functional design, and perhaps adding new curtains and lampshades, you can create an entirely new room for little or no money.

Perhaps arrange the furniture to face the window or the fireplace (if you have one), or arrange it in clusters to create "conversation centers." This third option could be especially useful if you entertain frequently. Clusters can create a warm and inviting feeling. Also, make good use of alcoves and windows—Julie Morgenstern says that the space surrounding windows is often the most underused space in a home. Could you install bookshelves surrounding the windows, or a low bookcase behind the sofa?

Clarify the overall purpose and main functions of your living area, and then consider which living-room furniture pieces you currently own, and which you're interested in adding, based on your needs. For furniture, less is more, so choose pieces that will be best utilized within the room. Could you purchase a coffee table or ottoman that opens up to reveal storage? A sofa that contains a stow-away bed for guests? Especially if you live in a small space, you'll want to think in terms of furniture that can meet a variety of needs.

Organizing Your Entertainment

If you'd like to keep your television and related items in an entertainment center, keep in mind that finding the best spot for such a large item is not always easy. When choosing a wall unit or entertainment center, first inventory all of the electronics that you plan to store on and in it. Does this piece of furniture have ample room for your equipment—television, cable box, DVD player, VCR, stereo, video-game system(s), surround-sound system, and speakers (left, right, and middle)? Are there enough electrical outlets located in the area? Will the unit hide all of the wires that go with your electronics? Be sure, too, that any furniture that will house electronics is well ventilated, as electronics produce a fair amount of heat.

After your entertainment center/wall unit is in place and you begin to add your various pieces of audio and video electronics, be sure to label all of the wires associated with each piece of equipment. Use a Brother P-Touch label maker (available from any office-supply store) or a pen to write labels on tape that can be wrapped around each wire. You can use different colored ties to wrap related wires together for easy identification.

Living-Area Storage Tips

Storage in the living area can be a tricky thing. Today, we have plenty of physical media to contend with, and in large part, it's that media that makes the mess. Big-time clutter comes from too many videos, DVDs, CDs, and games, and no good place to contain them. Take Charlie, a sound-hound in New Jersey. In the TV room of his pretty Dutch colonial home, he has got a hamper, a wicker chest, and an entire breakfront filled with compact discs. That's not all. He also has a bookcase crammed with old record albums. Talk about mass media! Charlie admits he probably listens to less than a third of the music in his collection, but discarding even a few? That's a thought too horrible to contemplate, and so the vinyl and discs continue their domestic incursion.

The most important element of a streamlined media room is managing your music and video collections. For CDs, DVDs, video games, and videocassettes, you can purchase a display rack/organizer that holds your entire collection. This can be a freestanding unit, one that is mounted on a wall, or one that fits in your entertainment center or wall unit. If it's a freestanding unit, you might place it in an unused corner of a room so that you can better utilize this space.

You may also want to invest in a multifunctional, universal remote control so that you can replace the separate remotes for your TV, cable box, VCR, etc., with one unit. An alternative is to place a remote-control caddy on the coffee table or near the TV, to help you keep track of your different remote-control units.

However, as with any other organizational project, this one starts with triage. Haul out four boxes and mark them KEEP, DONATE, DISCARD, and PRESERVE. Determine what you need to store, and then be creative.

Save Your Special Memories

The box marked PRESERVE is for all videos and music with special meaning. Make sure each is clearly labeled. How many times have you heard about someone accidentally taping over a precious graduation ceremony or once-in-a-lifetime music recital? Whenever you have precious memories saved on multimedia items, it's a good idea to have a duplicate copy made. All media has an army of adversaries: fingerprints, scratches, heat, dust. If a recording is really important to you, don't take chances with it. Make a backup and transfer it to the most up-to-date format available. Put old music cassette tapes on CD, videotapes onto DVD, and so on. Segregate these special tapes, CDs, and DVDs, and keep them together for safekeeping.

The Bottom Line

According to the Consumer Electronics Association, the average household is stocked with 100 CDs, more than forty DVDs, and sixteen video games. How does your home compare?

Decide What to Toss

Now that you've put aside the things with sentimental value, everything else is up for grabs. In with the new? Then it's out with the old. Take a fresh look at your entire entertainment library, from your old super-eights to your eight-tracks to the boxed DVD set you bought and never watch. Keep in mind that your collection is always going to grow. There will always be a new movie to buy, a CD you've got to have, and a new format coming down the pike that will make you want to go out and start your collection of all-time favorites all over again. With those things in mind, review your stash and ask yourself how you can start whittling it down to a manageable size. Here are a few ideas:

- Donate all redundant copies. If you have *The Godfather* on DVD, lose the VHS version. Ask a senior citizens' center if it might want a few additions to its video library.

- Find new homes for those movies you received as gifts and never liked. Why keep them around if you have no intention of watching them?

- Recycle all the children's movies your family has outgrown. Hospitals, nurseries, schools, and even the day-care center at the gym will be grateful recipients.

- Pass along the exercise videos you no longer use. The local recreation center could have a use for them.

- Throw out all the instructional videos and CDs that came with your ionizer, exercycle, bread maker ... you get the point. Somehow they seem to linger on the shelves long after the products they accompanied were discarded.

- Trash or transfer everything on dying, obsolete, or inconvenient-to-watch formats, like your original home movies.

Of course, this is also the time to chuck any old electronic equipment you might have lying around the room, too. Patricia, a mother of three, tried to do just that when she put an old television set down by the curb for garbage day pickup. Before the trash collectors could get to it, a neighborhood "recycler" had loaded the set into his van and wasn't too shy about ringing her doorbell and asking for the remote!

Word to the Wise

Turn your monitor into a photo album. Plug the memory card or stick from your digital camera into the TV or connect the cable from your camera to the set's USB port, and you'll be able to view your photographs on a nice big screen.

Organize Your Keepers

Now sort your CDs and videos using a system that makes sense for you. For some households, that might mean categorizing them by "owner," with Dad's movies in one section, Mom's favorites in another, and Junior's in a third. Or simply take a tip from your local video store and categorize them by format (video, DVD) and then by genre, like so:

- Comedy

- Drama

- Horror

- Sci-Fi

- Foreign

- Documentary

- Classics

- Children

- Instructional

Then, finally, sort videos alphabetically by title. Arrange CDs alphabetically by artist. Good job. So now where does your trimmed-down collection go? Depending on the quantity, you can repurpose a bookshelf, build shelves, or buy ready-made storage holders. Figure out if you have a preference for opened or closed storage. Many people who treasure their collections enjoy showing them off where others can see them.

Accordion-shaped units grow as your collection grows. They're expandable, wall-mountable, and some sleek models are as much about art as they are about utility. This storage option works for many types of media and doesn't eat up any floor space, either; if you've got a small room, it could be your answer. Modular systems are another approach for using the space you have now and having a plan for adding on later. Closed-door cabinets keep your music and movies dust-free and convey a cleaner look.

Ottomans with media storage beneath the seat offer unexpected storeroom space. Some oversize ottomans can hold hundreds of cassettes and DVDs. If you want guests to do a double take, buy a piece of furniture that does double-duty. Pedestal media holders are a perfect place to showcase a sculpture, vase, or plant. Better still for the storage savvy, they open up to reveal hidden shelves for all your movies.

Baskets make CDs and DVDs easy to access and, just as important, easy to put away. If you use baskets or drawers for storage, make sure the discs are stacked vertically, not on top of each other, so that you can read the titles.

You don't necessarily need to store all your media together. If you have a big collection of Christmas movies and CDs, for instance, you might want to put them with your holiday gear—as long as climate conditions are media-friendly. There's no reason the holiday classics you listen to one month a year should take up space on your shelves year-round.

Displaying Artwork and Collectibles

Displaying a collection of artwork, statues, trinkets, memorabilia, or collectibles can be tricky, especially in limited space. Begin by going through your collection and throwing away items that are broken or that you no longer wish to keep. Next, pick out any items that you want to store, but don't want to display at present. You want to avoid making your display look cluttered, because this won't be visually appealing. For the most dramatic visual impact, display just a few items that you really love. Don't be afraid of white space on the walls, either. White space can give the eyes a welcome break from visual clutter and can make a room feel larger.

When hanging pictures or artwork, try to keep them at eye level, and group them fairly closely together. Large gaps between artwork can sometimes be unattractive—instead of creating a feeling of space, the white between images can appear as "dead space."

Make sure your collections or items are properly lit and that the display you create is visually appealing and lacks clutter. According to some interior designers, the secret to elegant displays—even when working with everyday objects—is lush layering. To create your own elegant displays, begin with one tall object that you place in the center of the collection, and then loosely create a triangle shape as you add progressively shorter items to the display. If the items need wall space to be displayed, you might want to fill a blank wall with multiple items with a similar theme (in matching frames, or frames that are similar in style).

Personal Libraries

Some people choose to place personal libraries in the living area. This can be done with relative ease by installing bookcases and/or shelving for this purpose. Your bookcases can be freestanding units, or you can have a bookcase or shelving built directly into a wall. Be sure that the shelving can support the weight of the books. If bookcases seem unstable, you can bolt them to the wall.

To create a well-organized personal library, begin by sorting through your entire collection. Weed out books you no longer want and give them away to friends or donate them to a local library, thrift shop, or hospital.

Word to the Wise

Take care when arranging your bookshelves. Try grouping books of a similar category together. Likewise, oversized books do not require their own shelves. They can be placed on their side so that more shelves can fit into a smaller space.

Keep in mind that books do not need to fill your entire case. A little empty space in a bookshelf can provide a feeling of spaciousness or create an opportunity for variety—you could place a small sculpture on your bookcase, for example. Also, by leaving some empty space in your bookshelf, you convey to yourself and your family that there is still room to grow—your bookcase can accommodate the needs of a growing family and growing minds.

As you bring order and comfort to your living room, keep in mind that the best way to keep the space orderly is to make sure that you've integrated logical, easily accessible "homes" for all the items that you'll keep in there. As long as you have an easy spot to store items, the clutter won't accumulate. Careful planning and a little bit of maintenance each day will ensure that this space continues to be inviting and restful.

Chapter 7

Bathroom Basics

UTILITARIAN AND UTOPIAN. Can a bathroom really function as both? It's the place of prework traffic jams, where the inevitable time crunch forces us to play beat-the-clock every morning with the efficiency of an office manager. In a perfect world, it's also the place to unwind at the end of the day with, perhaps, a long soak in a spa-like ambiance. That's asking an awful lot of a single room, especially when you add in all the stuff we need to keep the place spic 'n span.

Thankfully, while the bathroom can easily fall into disarray, there are some steps you can take to get it in order and to make regular maintenance simpler. This chapter offers tips for making your bathroom more functional, attractive, and appealing—a place where you will want to linger and where your guests will feel welcome.

Appreciate Your Bathroom

Because many people work long hours and rush through their morning and evening rituals, the bathroom can easily become messy. The incredible variety of toiletries available only complicates the problem, as most bathrooms have cupboards full of half-used toothpaste tubes, shampoo bottles, and other personal-grooming products. It can be tempting to buy more of these products than we actually need, because they all promise something different. If you have difficult hair or skin, the temptation only increases, along with those half-full bottles littering the bathroom closet and cabinets.

For most people, it can be a challenge to find time to sort through the clutter and to keep the bathroom sparkling. Your bathroom, however, doesn't need to invite chaos. Nor should you feel like cringing when guests ask to use it. By taking just a few moments each day to order that space, it can be transformed from a place of chaos and clutter into a restful, serene retreat.

Be Attentive to Little Things

You do not need to remodel your bathroom to make it presentable. Instead, focus on being attentive to the little things when you're in there—be honest with yourself about what you want to keep and what you want to let go of, and learn to squeeze short cleaning segments into your regular trips into the bathroom.

Word to the Wise

Two-in-one and even three-in-one personal care products can free up space in your medicine cabinet. You can pick up razors with built-in shaving cream dispensers. Shampoo and conditioner combos have been around a while, but now you can add in body gel to the mix for a one-size-washes-all cleansing solution. A multipurpose body moisturizer can also be used for baby bottoms, cuticles, and calloused feet.

Because keeping the bathroom orderly can be a huge challenge, try to break the work down into small, manageable steps. Make bathroom maintenance a regular part of your routine and it will become less burdensome for you. Remember what the FlyLady says: "Even imperfect housework blesses my family."

Taming Toiletries

You'll need to clear things out first in order to clear things up. Begin with the basics: toiletries. Most people have a cumbersome collection of toiletries that they just don't use. Perhaps you purchased an expensive shampoo a year ago that did not work for your hair, but guilt has caused you to hold on to it. If it doesn't work for you, clear it out! Grab a beach blanket or old bed-sheet to put down on the floor. That'll be your temporary staging area. The guck from medicine cabinet and bathroom closet potions is laden with oils and syrupy goos you don't want to have to scrub up from your floors after your purging is done.

Starting with one section at a time, clear out your medicine chest, drawers, bathtub area, shelves, and so on. Inspect each item carefully. Have a supply of giant trash bags on hand for refuse, not the little supermarket bags. Think *big* and follow these tips to ensure a successful bathroom reorganization:

- **Look for expiration dates on medications and discard any drugs beyond their dates.** You may be tempted to eke out another dose, but expired medicines can lose their potency or, worse, make you ill. Add to your discard pile leftover antibiotics and medicines that aren't clearly labeled. This is one area where you don't want to take chances.

- **Open up any opaque containers to see exactly how much product is left inside.** There's no reason to hog up a lot of shelf space if a jar or bottle has only trace amounts left. Transfer remainders to smaller containers or consolidate half-empties of like products together.

- **Throw out any items you've tried and nixed.** This includes colognes, hair gels, makeup. You're not going to recoup your investment by having these things sit around collecting dust. Face it: The money's already gone.

- **Trash any products that are impractical for your lifestyle.** For example, that face mask that promises fountain-of-youth results if you wear it an hour a day, three times a week. It ain't gonna happen.

- **Discard old makeup that's been junking up your cosmetic bag.** Its purity may be compromised. Liquid makeup stays good for about a year, but figure on six months for eyeliner and three months for mascara. Otherwise, you run the very real risk of serious eye infections.

- **Get rid of that collection of makeup bags.** You know! The ones that come "free with purchase" at the cosmetic counter. You don't need them. Trust us.

- **Be realistic about your shower products.** Are all those shampoos, conditioners, hair masks, and body shampoos really necessary? Wouldn't one of each suffice? Back brushes, pumice stones, loofahs, nail brushes—use 'em or lose 'em. One woman came face to face with a little compulsion only after seeing the stockpile of moisturizers in her collection. Apparently, she never met a lotion she didn't like.

What can you do about an overabundance of products that might someday, in the distant future (when you have more time), improve your life? If you have more than you can realistically use, consider making a donation to others who can use the product right now. Homeless shelters can use shampoos and toiletries all the time, so bag up all that extra stuff and drop it off at your local shelter!

The Bottom Line

The Freecycle Network (*www.freecycle.org*) is an online grassroots organization made up of communities around the globe that allow individuals to recycle their no-longer-wanted goods by offering them free to other members. The website was started in 2003 to promote waste reduction. Post details on the items you want to get rid of, and chances are you'll have an enthusiastic taker before you know it.

Keep it Simple

As you shop for toiletries, try to practice no-net-gain. If you buy a new bottle of shampoo, throw out a mostly used old one. If you buy a new tube of toothpaste, get rid of the tubes you're not using. Ideally, every time you place something new in your cabinet, you'll take something out, so that you're not increasing the bathroom bulk each time you shop. Also, the less you keep in your bathroom cabinet, the better. While you'll need room for essentials, a disorganized cabinet can cause you to purchase items that you already have. You want to be able to open the cabinet door and quickly assess both what you have and what you need.

Bath-Linen Organization

After you've had an opportunity to clean out cabinets, closets, and under the sink, think about smart ways to store your towels and washcloths. If they often end up on the floor, this might be because you haven't simplified storage enough. Some towel racks are a hassle—they aren't anchored properly in the wall, so they slip off if any family member grabs them roughly, or they require that you carefully fold the towels to hang them. If you know that you simply don't have the time or inclination to labor over your towel racks, consider a simpler approach.

For example, hooks are a great way to keep your towels. Instead of having to stop and fold your towels, you can simply drop them on the hooks. Hooks require no uniformity and no formality, yet a line of towels hanging on hooks can look reasonably tidy. Just make sure that you install enough hooks so that each family member can fit a towel on a hook without straining the anchors in the wall. Wet towels can be heavy, so you want to be sure to properly attach the hooks to the wall.

Another option with towels is to buy two cubes or bins. In one bin, you can neatly fold towels that haven't yet been used. This cube filled with unused towels can be as lovely as it is practical. The other cube could be used as a hamper for used towels. Especially if your towels are all the same color, this kind of touch can add aesthetic appeal to your bathroom, while increasing function.

Watch Out!

You might need to label some hooks "Fresh towels" and others "Just used." You can also assign a hook to each member of your household. You might even want to designate a "guest" hook. While you may feel comfortable using the same towel for a few days, you don't want to accidentally give a guest a towel that isn't fresh.

General Bathroom Storage

When organizing your bathroom's cabinets, begin by taking everything out and dividing the contents into defined categories—prescription medications, nonprescription medications, first-aid supplies, hair-care products, makeup, toiletries, and so on. Take mental notes about what kind of organizational accessories may be useful.

The items that you use every day should be placed in a prominent, easily accessible location. If you have a cabinet under the sink, utilize this storage space for items that aren't used daily or that are too large to fit in a medicine cabinet or on the bathroom counter, such as cleaning supplies, extra toiletries, and your hair dryer.

The Medicine Cabinet

As we said previously, make sure any outdated prescriptions and over-the-counter medications have been thrown away. But in addition to medications, go through and purge any items that haven't been used for a year. When the cabinet is empty, clean the shelves and the interior, and then return everything in an easy-to-find order. Separate each family member's prescription medications and place them on separate shelves. Likewise, put all of the over-the-counter medications on a separate shelf. Group all similar items together so that they can be found quickly. There is nothing worse than scrounging for Advil when your head is pounding. Organizing your medicine cabinet is just one more way to care for yourself and your family.

Bulky Items

Your bathroom is not the best storage place for bulky items, such as tissues, toilet paper, diapers, and storage containers filled with extra bathroom items. All of these items can be stored at the bottom of your linen closet. By organizing your space efficiently, you may be able to buy larger quantities of certain items that you use frequently, saving yourself time, money, and trips to the store.

Clever Storage

After you've had a chance to purge and clean, it might be clear that you do need some additional bathroom storage. As you explore storage options, think outside the box. While you could purchase a shelving and cabinetry unit to go over your toilet, you might also be able to use a piece of furniture from another part of the house. Just keep in mind that any items used in your bathroom will need to be moisture resistant. Wood furniture can be used if it is well sealed.

Install Cubbies

A slightly more complex way to increase your bathroom storage is to install cubbies. This project will likely require the assistance of a professional carpenter, but the cubbies can be both useful and attractive. A cubby can be installed by cutting a hole into your existing wall. Often, there is a good deal of wasted space inside the walls of your bathroom. You can create shallow cubbies by cutting into the walls, or you can create deeper cubbies by cutting into an existing closet or storage space.

If you place neatly folded towels, plants, or other items in your cubbies, they can become attractive and functional additions to your bathroom. Exposed cubbies do run the risk, however, of causing some headaches, as they become just one more space to keep clean and dusted. You might want to install built-in cabinets that have doors so that you don't have to fret over them.

Shelving

Over-the-toilet shelving is a solution for ultratight spots. And think of the toilet tank as an extra shelf, too. Apothecary jars are great places to store items that don't have a logical home, such as manicure items, cotton balls, and dental accessories. Add a few hooks to the underside of a standard shelf and you have a place to hang hand towels. Install a peg or two on the wall by the sink for hairdryers and curling irons. They take up way too much space in a drawer. Wall-mounted hairdryers, often seen in hotel rooms, are another alternative.

Watch Out!

If you're considering a bathroom renovation, your designer may be qualified, but ask if he's also certified as a CBD (certified bathroom designer), an AKBD (associate kitchen and bath designer) or CMKBD (certified master kitchen and bath designer). That will let you know he's passed muster with the industry's stringent professional requirements.

The Beauty of the Basics

Although many items that you use every day—such as cotton balls, Q-tips, and washcloths—do not seem so lovely at first glance, you don't necessarily need to tuck these items away. For a very small amount of money, you can purchase matching glass jars to store them in. If they are displayed in a set of similar jars, they can have a cohesive, attractive look.

Not only will having these items out on a counter or exposed on a shelf be practical and time saving for you, but these little things can look quite lovely when they're displayed properly. Think about old-fashioned general stores, where all of the items were neatly displayed behind glass. When kept tidy and fairly uniform, the items in the jars provided interest for the eye and an overall effect that was appealing. Just keep in mind that only a very few essentials merit this kind of display. Many items are just too unattractive and clunky to fit the bill.

Finishing Touches

If you've followed the steps in this chapter, your bathroom has probably become a lot more functional and a good deal more attractive. Now it's time to think about the "glory work." Add some finishing touches to this space that has already become more appealing.

After you've settled into a routine of basic, regular bathroom maintenance, you might want to add in a few extra steps. For example, by rubbing the tub faucet with a dry, clean towel, you can make the metal shine. This small task only takes a few minutes, but will dramatically increase the beauty of your bathroom.

Likewise, you can bring some of the natural world into your bathroom. You can purchase hanging candleholders and place these on an untiled wall near the tub. You can alternate tea-light candles with fresh flowers from the garden for a simple, refreshing look. Or, you might bring in some fragrant plants that thrive in moist environments.

While the warm, moist atmosphere of many bathrooms can make mold a challenge, this climate can also be an opportunity to try out some tropical plants that would not necessarily thrive in other parts of the house. Many varieties of orchids, for example, can thrive in your bathroom.

As you tackle your bathroom, keep in mind that this project is ongoing and it doesn't have to be labor intensive. A little bit of regular maintenance can keep the larger messes at bay. Encourage yourself to be consistent, but do not demand perfection. Just continue to take little steps each day toward making your bathroom a serene space where you live more fully, linger a little longer, and find the refreshment your soul and body need.

Chapter 8

Beautiful Bedrooms

BEDROOMS ARE THE MARRIAGE OF PRACTICALITY AND SANCTUARY. They've become the go-to place to escape the stresses of everyday life. That holds true for kids, tweens, teens, and adults. The bedroom is the nap center, the reading room, the music salon, and, for many, the TV room. But where does the stuff for all those activities go? How do we squeeze it all in one place? We want it all, but having it all creates clutter zones in our sweet retreats.

Because of the frantic pace of life, bedrooms tend to be some of the most neglected rooms in the house. In the daily rush, clothes get piled on chairs, pillows are tossed in all directions, and by the end of the week people have to dig a path to find their bed. But this is not the way a bedroom has to be. At the end of a long day, your bedroom can be a place of quiet and refreshment. This chapter will explore ways to make the most of your sleeping space—how to organize your clothing, select and care for linens, and how to create a bedroom that is conducive to rest and nourishing for your soul.

Out of Sight

Ah, pity Karen, a harried homeowner in Myrtle Beach, South Carolina, who wishes her bedroom could be an oasis of tranquility. You've heard of junk drawers? Hers is a junk room. The thing is that she's honest enough to admit it's the very definition of disorganization. A jumble of clothing is the main offender—and not just her clothes and her husband's. Their teenage daughter's jeans and T-shirts have managed to migrate into the master bedroom, too. And that's not all. The room is filled with unwanted Christmas gifts that still need to be returned, plus fabric scraps, wrapping paper, party decorations, even bubble wrap. It has all the makings of a craft room—but in the wrong room. Karen says with an exasperated sigh, with all that clutter, it's not easy to dust or vacuum. Her husband, Paul, is not much better. He empties his pockets out every evening, piling receipts, business cards, gum wrappers, and who knows what else on the dresser rather than in the trash. Paul is her buddy in grime. Every weekend, Karen promises herself she'll tackle the mess, but then she gets so overwhelmed by not knowing where to start that she doesn't start at all. Sound familiar?

Reclaim Your Sanctuary

It's easy enough to shut the door on an untidy den or ignore the five-cart pile-ups in the basement, but it's impossible to dismiss the room you spend so many waking hours in, not to mention all your sleeping hours. If you're routinely stepping over clothes to get from one side of the room to the other or peeling evidence of the day's activities off your bed before tucking in for the night, it's time to stop the madness. Close your eyes and take a minute to imagine how you would feel about your bedroom if every article of clothing was in its rightful place, every ragtag trinket had a home, and every loose piece of paper was neatly tucked away in a folder where it belonged. Even if your bedroom took months or years to get into the dire shape it's in, it only takes a heavy-duty roll-up-your-sleeves session or two to convert bedlam back to bedroom.

How do you *use* your bedroom? Is it strictly for sleeping, readying for work, and personal time? Is it the place you while away the hours watching TV? Does it stand in as spillover for the kids' playroom? Masters of multitasking find it hard to set limits and form boundaries. If the latter describes your room, no doubt your décor reflects that, too. Look around. Could your interior design style be described as "Disney vacation meets office supply store?" "Romantic chic meets Main Street Dry Cleaners?" And if the answer is yes, is that really the aesthetic you want to have in your haven?

Word to the Wise

According to Ariane Benefit, professional organizer and president of OrganizingforHealth.com, one key to clearing out clutter is to devise storage solutions that are every bit as easy to use as no solutions. In other words, you can remedy the problem by making it just as convenient to put your clothes away as it is to throw them on the floor.

The most important reason to make your bedroom a refuge is to give you a place to unwind, meditate, pray, sleep, and relax—in other words, to make it the place you shake off the anxieties and pesky irritations of the day. If your bedroom is a jumble of disorder, it stands to reason your equilibrium will be undermined. You roll over in bed, and piles of unpaid bills are staring you in the face shouting Pay Me! Pay Me! Overdue work evaluations on the dresser are joining in the deal-with-me chorus. Feel-good books and inspirational reading is fine. Business manuals? There are more appropriate places for them. Is it any wonder why 35 million Americans complain of chronic insomnia? Don't let the world come knocking at your bedroom door. If you're surrounded by clutter, it just follows that negative energy is going to interfere with relaxation.

To Your Health

One thing all health professionals agree on is the importance of a good night's sleep. Even exercise machines like treadmills and stationary bicycles can attract the wrong kind of energy that can sabotage rest.

Everything in the bedroom should be geared to support sleep. Get rid of the phone, or at least turn the ringer off at night. If you're the kind of person who stays up nights running the same thoughts through your brain over and over again—What am I going to wear to work tomorrow? What time is that staff meeting?—prepare the night before. Make a to-do list, and lay out your clothes. Do whatever it takes to get the worries off your mind so you can unwind. A serene, relaxing bedroom setting helps you end the day with ZZZZZs instead of GRRRRRs.

An Organized Inquiry

What is feng shui? Feng shui is the ancient Chinese practice of living harmoniously with the natural elements and forces of the Earth. Practitioners believe that orienting and arranging objects in certain ways can enhance the positive energy flow of a given space, promote health and prosperity, and result in a clutter-free environment.

According to organizer Ariane Benefit, bedroom clutter can impact your health in other ways, too. For one thing, if surfaces are covered, chances are any cleaning effort is going to be cursory at best. Many people have symptoms of chronic sinus conditions that can be traced to the fact they're spending seven, eight, nine, or more hours sleeping in a dust-filled environment. Dust bunnies, balls of cat hair—some rooms are a virtual menagerie of irritants.

Fortunately, the plan to master your master bedroom is easy. Just take it one step at a time!

Take a Clothing Inventory

Most people have a good deal more in their dressers and closets than they actually need. This is especially the case with women, who may have as many as four different sizes of clothing because their bodies shrink and expand. Many women hold on to "skinny clothes" with the dream that they'll one day fit back into them, while also resigning themselves to the reality of those not-so-skinny clothes that also need to be kept, just in case surprise expansions occur.

Overstuffed drawers and closets, however, create headaches. Finding clothing in the morning can be a huge hassle. The last thing you need when you're struggling against the clock is to have to sift through piles of wrinkly clothing. If you can thin down the contents of your dressers and closets, however, you'll find that getting ready in the morning is a breeze. You may even find that you don't need to go shopping after all. Perhaps all that you need is actually tucked away in your drawers, just waiting to be rediscovered.

While the idea of organizing your clothing may feel overwhelming, you can break the task down into small steps—perhaps you could try to tackle just one drawer a day (or even a week). As the FlyLady says, "Progress, not perfection, is the goal." As long as you're making steady (even if slow) progress, you're going to begin to feel better about your room.

As you sift through your drawers, set out two boxes, one for "Giveaway/Sell" items, and another for "Store" items. Try to be as realistic as possible. If you haven't been able to fit into your size 4 jeans for a good three years, you might want to let them go, trusting that should you shrink again, you'll certainly be able to replace them—and you'll have a great time doing it!

The Bottom Line

The organization Vietnam Veterans of America (*www.vva.org*; 800-775-8387) will pick up items right from your front door. The group accepts clothing, small appliances, bric-a-brac, small furniture, televisions, lamps, bedding, and more as long as it's in good, workable condition.

Find places other than the closet for storing clothing that you know you'll need but won't be using for several months, such as winter coats, thick sweaters, and other seasonal items. Ideally, you'll move these items to the basement, attic, or storage each time spring rolls around. This small step will simplify your life and help you to feel more at peace in your room.

If you live in a small space without an attic or basement, underbed storage may be an ideal way for you to tuck away off-season items, bedding, or other bulky items. Check stores such as Ikea (*www.ikea.com*) and The Container Store (*www.containerstore.com*) for different storage options. Keep in mind, however, that adding additional storage does come with temptation. You may be inclined to hold on to some items that you'll never use just because you've created space for them. Ideally, underbed storage will be reserved for items that will be useful to you (and that have proven their usefulness over the years).

Bedroom Hot Spots

You may have a few hot spots in your bedroom that could be eliminated. Perhaps there is a chair in the corner, intended for reading, that gets heaped with clothing on a regular basis. Consider moving this chair to a different part of the house so that you (and your loved ones) won't be tempted to drop clothing on it at the end of the day. Heaps of clothing will make you feel discouraged and tired, so it is best to remove furniture upon which clothing can accumulate.

Watch Out!

If you want a simple way to keep clothing off the floor and furniture, install a row of hooks in your closet. It takes just seconds a day to "hook" your clothes. With hooks, clothes are easy to spot and putting them away no longer feels like a chore. Take care not to overload your hooks and to only place items on them that will not become stretched as a result.

Removing furniture from your room can have a surprising side benefit. Not only will this make it easier to keep things tidy, but a little less furniture can go a long way toward making a small space feel more comfortable. Keep the primary uses of your bedroom in mind as you evaluate your furniture needs. Rarely used exercise equipment should be shown the door, because in addition to creating clutter, it might make you feel guilty every night as you're drifting off to sleep. Everyone feels burdened enough without the additional trigger of a StairMaster beside the bed. Ideally, the last thoughts of the day will be mellow ones, not thoughts like, "I haven't exercised in weeks. Why did I spend good money on that equipment that I never use?" When you're tired, those kinds of thoughts can be overwhelming, and they might make it harder to fall asleep.

Quick Drawers

Dresser drawers serve their purpose best when designated for specific roles. Store lingerie, socks, and underwear in one drawer, sweaters in another, sleepwear in a third, and workout clothes in a fourth. You get the idea. Without a system of organization, items just get thrown around without rhyme or reason. In short order, they get out of order. Sweaters, jeans, knitwear, and other items not prone to wrinkles are well suited to drawers. Hang garments made of rayon, linen, and cotton in closets, as well as pleated and creased items that need to keep their shapes.

Word to the Wise

Sweeten up your drawers and closets. Scented drawer liners are a nice touch. For a stronger scent, throw in those perfumed sample cards that come in department store catalogues and magazines. For something a bit subtler, toss in a small bar of fragrant soap or a sachet of fresh lavender.

To squeeze more into your drawers, roll up garments instead of stacking them. It's easier to see what you've got that way, too.

One more way you can help yourself keep things in check is also arguably the best way. If you buy something new, throw something out. Once you pare your wares down to size, this one-in, one-out philosophy ensures your possessions never get out of balance.

Drawers on the Floor

Think about drawers on the floor. If you've got a nice chunk of space down under the bed, exploit it. If you don't have the space, inexpensive bed-lifters are available that snap onto the legs of your bed to give you a few more inches of height. Made-to-fit roll-out drawers and plastic containers come in handy. Just make sure the plastic ones are see-through so you know what's in it without wasting time playing guessing games. Those heavy-duty plastic zip bags that blankets come in can be repurposed for storage, too. Consider using under-bed areas for seasonal items. Make sure whatever storage option you choose is airtight to keep out dust and pests. It could be weeks or months before you need to use those items again. Pass on storing things you use every day under there. It's just not practical. You don't want to have to get down on your hands and knees to search for commonly used items.

Vanity Fair

Don't forget to consider what's on top of your dresser. Wrist watches, earrings, and on-again, off-again rings? Tidy up the tabletop with a handsome jewelry box, just big enough to store your everyday gems. For men, a compartmented valet will hold the day's loose pocket change, keys, and watch. Dedicated watch valets can cradle multiple watches, protect them from scratches, and keep them dust free.

Instead of putting loose change on your dresser at the end of each day, toss your coins into a jar and watch your money grow. Automatic coin-rolling machines like the ones offered by Coinstar (*www.coinstar.com*) will tally up your totals for a small percentage fee. You can pocket the cash, donate it automatically to charity or, at certain locations, use the proceeds to purchase a no-fee gift card. Coinstar machines are available at retail outlets and supermarkets throughout the country.

Sock Therapy

Ah, the bane of our existence—the mighty sock. Or, more typically, the missing sock. Before you have to issue an all-points-bulletin, pick up plastic or cardboard organizer inserts to keep the sock drawer orderly and matches easy to find. Sock organizers also give drawers a custom-designed look at a bargain price. Sort socks by color. Is there anything more frustrating than trying to figure out in the dim light of morning if a pair is black, charcoal, or dark navy? Drawer organizer inserts, now commonly available, come in a variety of sizes, not just for socks but also for underwear, gloves, and lingerie. For pantyhose, some women swear by all-purpose zip-close baggies as an effortless and inexpensive way to arrange hose by color and protect them from snags.

The Great Escape

Remember, the hardest part of straightening out your bedroom is making the commitment to do so. Be inspired by the "after" picture in your head of a beautiful, streamlined room by taking charge of your stuff. Bedroom organization is all about balance and maintenance—not extremes. No one wants a bedroom that resembles an army barracks. This private space, separated from the communal areas of your house, is where you can feel the power of place. If you take a holistic approach, you'll see the benefits rippling through into other areas of life. Less household clutter leads to more effective cleaning, and that can lead to better health. Less mental clutter can lead to better sleep and enhanced vitality.

Once you start to see the top of your dresser again and the pattern of your carpeting, you know you're well on your way to having a room you'll no longer want to escape from, but a refuge you'll want to escape to.

Chapter 9

Gorgeous Guestrooms

IF YOU FREQUENTLY HOST GUESTS, then you know how chaotic it can feel when you're preparing for them. This chapter will explore ways to make your guests feel more comfortable in your home, as well as ways to put you at ease before (and during) their visit. If you take a well-organized approach to hosting guests, you'll be able to relax and enjoy their company—and they'll be able to relax and enjoy a peaceful retreat in your home.

Planning Ahead

If you've been slowly working through the steps in this book, then you're probably beginning to feel a little bit better about the idea of hosting guests. Sometimes people put off guests simply because they feel that their homes are not clean or attractive enough. You have no need for shame, though! Whatever you have been able to accomplish while slowly working through the steps in this book has most likely improved the look and feel of your home.

Keep in mind, as well, that few guests expect perfection (if you fear they will, you can suggest that they stay at a bed-and-breakfast). Because you live in your home with your family and pets, your home is going to show signs of life no matter how hard you work to keep it orderly. This is okay—your guests have come, at least in part, because they want to experience a bit of your life, imperfections and all. After all, they have the same challenges in their own homes.

Prioritizing

In Victoria Moran's book *Shelter for the Spirit*, she offers this tip for simplifying your life: "Put things with feelings first." Sometimes when you prepare for guests you can let yourself get so stressed about cleaning and cooking that you forget the people who presently surround you. But the attitude that you have about hosting guests will be conveyed to those who know you best. If you're short-tempered and tense, you will convey to your family that you don't really enjoy guests. If you can be calm and prepare for your guests a little bit each day, you're more likely to enjoy your guests and your children will be more likely to behave well when the guests are there.

Word to the Wise

Victoria Moran, on prioritizing: "Balancing your checkbook is probably not as important as listening to your child. Having a romp with the dog should usually take precedence over waxing the kitchen floor. That's because bank accounts and linoleum can wait until a more convenient time. Things with feelings cannot."

The frantic pace of life can make it difficult to plan ahead, but you'll never regret having taken small steps to prepare for guests. As much as you want to graciously host them, be realistic up-front about what is possible. If you live in a major city and have small children and an airport run seems next to impossible, let your guests know a few weeks in advance that they'll need to take a shuttle or taxi to your home. If you provide them with very specific instructions, they should have no problem doing this. It is far worse for guests to sense that they are a burden to you than it is for them to have to exercise some independence.

Watch Out!

When you plan meals for your guests, keep in mind any dietary restrictions they might have. If they have very specific food needs or preferences, you can take them to the grocery store when they arrive and allow them to be part of meal planning.

If you enjoy cooking and are confident that your guests can eat whatever you serve up, think in terms of make-ahead dishes that you can prepare early in the week and then warm for your guests. Homemade soup with good bread is an ideal choice for that first night, as you often won't know if your guests have eaten during the journey. Soup is light but satisfying, and if your guests have eaten, soup can wait until tomorrow.

Another great dish for guests that freezes well is lasagna. You can make this early in the week, freeze it, and then reheat it when your guests arrive. The best part of make-ahead meals is that you won't need to frantically clean (while cooking) just before your guests arrive. That challenge, especially when coupled with an airport run, is enough to make anyone tense!

Serve Local Fare

If you live in an area that is known for some particular food, try to serve that to your guest. If you live in New York, for example, and your guest enjoys fish, bring in fresh lox and bagels in the morning. If you live in Chicago, plan to take your guest out to enjoy Chicago-style pizza or an eatery in one of the many ethnic neighborhoods. If you live in

Oregon, by all means, serve fresh Pacific salmon—any guest from the East Coast will immediately realize that Pacific salmon offers a completely different culinary experience from its Atlantic counterpart.

The Bottom Line

Eating can be an adventure, especially for your houseguests. A.A. Milne wrote, "'When you wake up in the morning, Pooh,' said Piglet . . . , 'what's the first thing you say to yourself?' 'What's for breakfast?' said Pooh. 'What do *you* say, Piglet?' 'I say, 'I wonder what's going to happen exciting *today*?' said Piglet. Pooh nodded thoughtfully. 'It's the same thing,' he said."

A great way to show your guests local fare is to take them to a farmers' market that requires that all the farmers be local (keep in mind that many markets allow food that has been shipped in from faraway states). Local markets not only allow you the opportunity to connect with the people who plant and harvest the bounty on your table, but will let your guests see what types of produce, cheeses, and breads are produced right in your own backyard.

After you've thought out some meal possibilities, think in terms of snacks to keep around the house. Crackers, fresh veggies, cheese, fruit, and dip can be nice to munch with your guests while you catch up with them. Guests also sometimes wake hungry in the middle of the night— ideally, they will know which cupboard to dig into for a quick, satisfying snack. If you have the opportunity to bake something fresh before your guests arrive, all the better.

On that first evening with your guests, make sure that they know how the coffeemaker works and where the tea is stored. Show them where you keep cereal and fresh fruit. Some guests (especially those who have traversed time zones to get to you) will wake before you do. You don't need to rush out of bed to help them—just let them know where everything is the night before. They might even appreciate having a chance to wake slowly by themselves while you sleep.

Convertible Spaces

In most people's homes, space is tight. Many people are forced to host guests in the living room. If this is your situation, there are a few things that you can do to make your guests more comfortable. First, if you do purchase a sofa bed, don't go by aesthetics alone! Make sure that you have an opportunity to test the mattress before the purchase is final. If you've found a sofa that you love and is within your budget but you're not satisfied with the mattress, you can buy an extra mattress pad to increase the comfort. You can purchase a Tempur-Pedic mattress pad, or any foam pad at a discount or department store. These small touches can greatly increase your guests' ability to sleep in your home.

If you've designated a room to be your guest room, but you don't have guests too often, you probably want to utilize this space for other activities as well. Perhaps you'll use your guest room as a home office, an exercise room, a room to participate in your hobby, a room to display your knickknacks or collections, or a playroom. If the room does have multiple uses, it can be challenging to convert it into a guest space—the mere clutter most of these uses create can make the space feel cramped and unwelcoming.

Ideally, you'll decrease the clutter in that room. This will take vigilance on your part because you probably won't have to see the clutter all the time.

One of the greatest temptations with an "extra" room is that this room can easily become a catch-all for the items from the rest of your house that haven't yet found a home. If you plan to use this space for guests, however, you'll want to try your best to stay on top of the clutter. Otherwise, the prospect of guests will feel overwhelming.

If you'll also use this space as a home office or hobby area, think in terms of furniture that can conceal—for example, a desk/armoire that can be closed at the end of the working day is a great way to keep your working space private and to help you set boundaries on your time. When the desk is closed, work for the day has ended and you can relax with your family, just as those who travel to a different physical space are able to at the end of the day.

Create a Peaceful Retreat

Wherever your guests slumber, you'll want to make the space conducive to sleep. Even a living room can be a peaceful place to sleep if you keep a few things in mind. First, can you make your guest space dark enough? Many people sleep better in a dark room, especially in an unfamiliar setting. If you don't own any yet, consider purchasing thick curtains to block out streetlight.

Light that may not be bothersome to you could feel invasive to your guests, so be sure to seek creative ways to solve this problem. If thick curtains are outside of your current budget (or you simply don't like the look of them) you might purchase facemasks (to block out the light) and several pairs of earplugs for your guests. Especially if you have small children, your guests will thank you for those earplugs!

Just as some guests will want complete darkness, others will need a little bit of light. Offer a nightlight and alarm clock to your guest in case these items will be useful. Ideally, the room where the guests sleep will have a variety of light sources so that they can use lamplight to read by at night and brighter lights to dress by. Carefully selected lighting can help create a warm ambiance in almost any room.

The Pet Problem

If possible, keep your pets contained during the nights when you have a guest in your home. Pets wandering the house can be startling for a guest, especially if you have an overly friendly dog or cat that decides to curl up with your guest. Check with your guests to see how they feel about pets before they arrive and plan accordingly.

If your guest has a pet allergy, try to keep your pets away from her sleeping area. It is a good idea to vacuum up pet hair as much as possible, although take care to do this a few days in advance, as vacuuming can stir up dander and actually make it harder for allergic guests to breathe. At the very least, make sure that you have an allergy medication on hand should your guest need a little relief.

Comforting Touches

There are small things you can do that will make a big difference to your guest. In terms of bedding, try to provide your guests with the softest sheets you can afford. The higher the thread count, generally, the silkier the sheets will feel. Flannel sheets in winter are also a nice touch for guests.

Make sure to provide ample blankets for your guests so that they can layer and remove blankets as they see fit. It is best to provide at least two pillows per guest, especially because some people are very sensitive to the flatness or puffiness of particular pillows and it may take your guest some time to determine which pillow she can actually sleep on. Again, check with guests about allergies. Some people love the feel of down pillows, for example, while others will sniffle all night long if forced to sleep on a down pillow—if possible, purchase some allergen-free pillows for guests.

Word to the Wise

A vase of fresh-cut flowers near your guests' sleeping area can add a welcoming, elegant touch. Likewise, you can leave a stack of books that you feel they might enjoy on a table near the area where they'll sleep. Many people have trouble sleeping in a new space and will welcome the diversion.

Leave fresh towels (two for bathing and at least one washcloth) at the foot of your guest bed. This way, your guest will know that she has fresh and clean towels. If you purchase guest towels in a color other than the one your family usually uses, you will be better able to distinguish which towels are for guest use only.

Room for Guests

Even if you can't provide a separate sleeping space for guests, can you provide a few empty drawers or baskets under a coffee table or some closet space for them? Here is where all of your hard work begins to pay off. Instead of needing to clear out drawers and closet space for guests, you'll likely have some empty spaces just waiting to be filled. A little bit of space to unpack and settle in will allow your guests to feel more at home and will allow them to keep their clothes looking fresh and unwrinkled.

The Bottom Line

If closet space is tight, purchase a freestanding clothing rack from any hardware store or mass-market retailer. It's also nice if you can offer your guests a television and/or radio in the guest room.

Furnishing Your Guest Room

If you are in a position to purchase additional furnishings for the guest room, think carefully about what you'll be using this room for in addition to housing guests. Measure the room carefully, and then determine what type of furniture is required to make the room functional. As with all of the rooms in your home, take advantage of organizational products, such as specialty hangers, underbed storage bins, dresser drawers, and shelving to organize and properly store your belongings. To save space in your guest room, you may not want to use a full-size, traditional bed.

Keep in mind, however, that there are many space-saving alternatives, discussed in the following sections.

Air Mattress

The AeroBed (*www.thinkaero.com*) is an excellent choice. AeroBed is a self-inflating bed that fully inflates in less than a minute and deflates in fifteen seconds. It has a built-in electric pump for fast, easy inflation. When not in use, it deflates to the size of a sleeping bag and can be stored in a closet.

Futon

The biggest benefit of futons is that they're much more affordable than sofa beds. They're also generally far more sleep-friendly than traditional sofa beds, although they tend to not be as comfortable (or attractive) as sofas. Keep in mind that when unfolded, futons can take up the same amount of space as a full-sized couch or sofa bed.

Sofa Bed or Chair

When not used as a bed, these pieces of furniture double as full-sized couches or oversized armchairs that come in a wide range of styles. When a bed is needed, they typically unfold into a single-, king- or queen-sized bed. Some sofa beds have custom-size mattresses. The cost of sofa beds varies greatly, based on the quality of the couch as well as the type and quality of the mattress built into it.

Keep in mind that some sofa beds can be uncomfortable to sit and sleep on. They also tend to be heavy and extremely difficult to move. Should you choose to purchase a sofa bed, make sure you've inquired about the comfort of the mattress beneath the cushions. If you already own a sofa bed with an uncomfortable mattress, consider purchasing a generic memory foam mattress topper. This small addition could greatly improve your guests' sleep.

Portable Cot

These metal frames on wheels fold in half for easy storage in a basement and utilize a thin (often foam) mattress. They come in several different sizes and tend to be very inexpensive. Cots are a good option for children, but adults are likely to wake with a sore back after sleeping on them.

Wall Bed

If you're building a home office and want it to double as a comfortable guest room, Techline (*www.techlineusa.com*) offers a home-office furniture system that includes a pull-down wall bed. This system allows you to utilize the room space available to include a full-sized desk, shelves, cabinets, plus the pull-down bed that sets up in minutes. See Chapter 15 for additional information about setting up a home office.

Displaying and Organizing Photographs

Whether your guests sleep in the living room, a guest room, or your home office or hobby room, it is likely that your photographs will be stored somewhere near them. Perhaps they fill a guest-room closet or take up precious drawer space in your living room. In order to create a more orderly environment for your guests and yourself, you'll want to take some time to get your photographs in order.

You can display, organize, and store your personal photographs and memorabilia in many ways. Because you probably don't have enough wall space to frame and hang all of your pictures, consider a few alternatives, such as creating a scrapbook or using labeled boxes for storage.

Organizing Photos and Negatives

Begin by finding a method for organizing all of your photographs, including labeling the negatives, writing about the pictures, and storing the photographs until you are ready to mount them in your scrapbook. After you establish a method, every time you have a new roll of film developed, implement your organizational strategy immediately. You may make a rule to develop your photos within a week of taking them, for example, or to organize the photos in an album or photo box within a month of having them developed.

Also, there are a variety of things that you can purge out of your photo boxes without even having to deliberate. You don't need those floppy envelopes that photos come in, especially if you're going to use a shoebox or albums. Dump these excess items immediately and you'll be better able to sort through the photographs.

Watch Out!

Although it can be tempting to hold on to all of your photographs, extra photos just generate clutter. If you have duplicates of photos you love, send them to receptive friends and family. They'll enjoy the fact that you thought of them, and you'll have a few less objects to keep in order. Also, purge all photos that are blurry or unflattering to the subjects portrayed—your friends and family will thank you for this!

Make sure to keep your photos in a temperature-controlled environment. Basements and attics are unsafe places for photographs. Also, the way that you store your photographs will have a dramatic effect on their longevity. When possible, keep them in plastic bins. Use acid-free labels to date and describe photos. If you're able to store your photographs in a climate-controlled environment, consider professional home organizer Julie Morgenstern's method of using labeled shoeboxes. Shoeboxes don't cost anything and are the ideal size for photographs. You can arrange your photos in a variety of ways—by year, by topic, by vacation—or you can have bins for each member of your family (or each branch of your extended family). Even if you never get around to placing your photos in albums, a basic shoebox system can serve to make them accessible for years to come.

Organizing your photographs can be daunting, so don't try to tackle them all in an afternoon or over a weekend. Instead, make a weekly commitment to a manageable goal, such as creating one shoebox a week. You can even pencil your photo-organizing time into your calendar.

You might also want to create a simple box for pictures and keepsakes pertaining to each family member. These boxes will probably need to be larger than a shoebox if you want to save children's art, report cards, and other larger items. Be selective as you create your memento box. Choose only the best to keep—those that most clearly represent the phase your child is in and the progression of their abilities. Perhaps you'll want to limit yourself to one from each month. After several years of collecting small mementos, you can turn the contents of this box into an album.

Making Scrapbooks

After you've reviewed and organized all of your photos, choose your favorites for incorporation into your photo album or scrapbook. Choose an actual album or scrapbook that conveys a specific theme, such as family vacations, holidays, family memories, or childhood. After you've decided which album to begin with, determine the sequence of the album—chronological, by themes, or by events.

The number of photographs you can get on a page will depend on the page size, the size of the photographs, and how much you crop the background of the photographs. You can, of course, be creative and overlap your photographs.

Word to the Wise

Scrapbooking.com (*www.scrapbooking.com*) and BestScrapbookTips.com (*www.bestscrapbooktips.com*) offer countless ideas for creating a highly personalized scrapbook with your photographs and other memorabilia.

When you begin to place your photos in scrapbooks, take care to purchase only albums with acid-free pages that won't damage your photos. If you do use a glue stick, use only glue sticks that are designed for photographs. Also, you can attach newspaper clippings to the pages of your album with a similar washable, nontoxic glue stick. Plastic photo sleeves are ideal for putting photos into albums quickly and for quick, safe removal.

Converting to Digital Photos

The digital revolution is one of the greatest things that has happened to photo hoarders (and those who live with them). Instead of stacks and stacks of loose, unidentifiable photos, you can now store all of your photos on your computer and only print those you love.

In addition to taking digital photos, you can also convert your old photos to a digital system. You can use a scanner to scan your existing photos to create high-resolution electronic files on your computer's hard drive, on Zip disks, or on writable CD-ROMs. The Hewlett-Packard Photosmart photo scanner, for example, is relatively inexpensive and allows you to scan photos, negatives, or slides using any PC-based personal computer. When you want to develop photos, you can use an online service or have them developed at your regular retail developer.

Watch Out!

Save time now by immediately deleting photos from your camera—any photo that is out of focus can be trashed. Also, if you take a series of photos of a place or person, just choose your favorite and delete the rest. On a digital camera, there is no waste.

Many of these services also offer the option of creating photo books or calendars. These photo books can make a great gift for friends and family, and they provide a quick, easy way to create albums with the click of your mouse.

Back Up all Digital Images

Although most people have heard that digital images should be backed up, few people actually create backup files. If your entire archive of images is dependant upon your computer, however, you are in a vulnerable position. Computers can be destroyed in an instant by fire, flood, lightning, or hard-drive failure, and with the loss of your computer, you could easily lose a lifetime of photographs. An easy backup method is to create CDs with your images and store them in a different part of your home.

Whether you're creating back-up for your photographs or preparing your home for guests, every bit of planning helps. By taking steps to organize and plan for your guests, you can create an environment that is restful for them and peaceful for you. No matter where your guests sleep, you can make them feel comfortable by paying attention to small details and adding comforting touches to their sleeping space. When it comes to guests, a little bit of thoughtfulness in advance goes a long way.

part 3

bring it to light

Closets. Laundry rooms. Attics. Basements. What do they have in common? Most people never see these spaces in your house—and it's not like you're spending a lot of time there either. Because these spaces offer concealment, it can be tempting to stuff them full with mismatched items. However, what goes in must, of course, come out. But it often doesn't come out quite as one might hope—instead of an organized collection of board games, tools, and laundry, you open the doors only to have an avalanche of Monopoly money, screws, and towels come crashing down on your head. This section offers practical solutions for ordering your spaces that don't usually see the light of day—and better caring for the items in them—one space at a time.

Chapter 10

Customize Your Closets

DOES YOUR CLOTHES CLOSET LOOK LIKE A DEPARTMENT STORE SALES RACK the day after Christmas . . . you know, where everything's in a kind of helter-skelter, nothing-quite-makes-sense disarray? Do you need to send in a search party to find your favorite shirt? Instituting an organizational system beefed up with a few space-saving solutions can bring order and breathing room to even the smallest of closets. Even if you think there's just not enough room, a few nips and tucks can result in a streamlined closet makeover.

Breaking Out of the Rut

Facing a dysfunctional closet every morning is a bad way to start the day. Life is filled with anxieties, many of which are out of one's control. This is one that's definitely in your control. Purging your clothes closets of unworn and unwearable apparel and ridding your hall closets of rarely used gear gets at the heart of your home's storage capabilities. Tackle it, and you'll not only maximize your space, you'll feel empowered as you face your day.

The Bottom Line

According to California Closets, the cost of a custom storage system can range in price from $400 to $30,000, with the average sale around $2,900. California Closets has installed more than 4 million custom-designed storage systems around the world since its founding in 1978.

So let's get down to the biggest offenders. At the top of the list: adding a new item of clothing or pair of shoes without purging any of the old ones. It stands to reason that you'll max out your capacity in no time. And one more thing: When you've got so much packed in, it's impossible to keep track of what's there. So what happens? You wind up buying multiples of what you've already got.

Retail Therapy

One main of the main reasons that closets tend to be a problem is that shopping for clothes is a national pastime. There's a reason it's called retail therapy. It's fun and, hey, it makes us feel good—up to a point, that is. When the shopping bags come home and there's no place to put the goods, those feel-good moments turn into stressful ones.

Finally, the closet winds up being the place most frequently used to throw stuff into when we need to quickly tidy up for company. But when company's gone, the closet catch-all is never "undone."

Word to the Wise

Special-occasion clothes like formal suits, gowns, and party dresses might stay in your closet for years without getting a wearing. It's a good idea to try on these outfits at least once a year to make sure they still deserve a place in your closet. Fashions change, weight shifts. It may no longer be the great number you remember.

Straighten It Out

Don't worry though! Putting a clothes-storage system in place is easier than you think, no matter what size closet you've got or how busy it is. Some people might argue that small-closet organization is an oxymoron. Rest assured there are entire businesses created around the concept of decluttering closets, and size is no barrier. You don't need to break down walls and make a bigger closet when you could make a smarter closet. Closet pros are available and happy to turn your muddled mess into a designer showcase with generous built-ins that look like fine furniture. Or you can make it a do-it-yourself project with a game plan and the help of a few space-saving devices. So let's find out exactly what's going on with—and what's going into—those closets of yours.

Time to Face the Closet

Okay—before you proceed, take a deep breath and a moment to think. Remember that you're not going to organize all your closets today. Plan to take just one step toward your goal of orderly closets.

You may want to make a list of the closets in your home that are particular hot spots. Before you head into battle, you'll need a plan. Assess the closets throughout your home—how long would it take to organize each one? Are some closets a priority? Consider how your life is affected by the different closets in your home—perhaps the chaos in your bedroom closet affects you more than the other ones.

After you decide that your closets are in need of reorganization and how long it will take to tackle each one, create a realistic schedule for your efforts. Just as you've done in other parts of your home, you'll want to create three boxes so that you can quickly sort through your belongings. Give these boxes any name you'd like, but the gist of the titles are "Give away/Sell," "Throw away," and "Decide later."

Shun Diversions

Now is not the time for long deliberations about what to keep and what to let go of. Now is also not the time for paging through old scrapbooks, clipping your fingernails (when you finally find that clipper!), or trying clothes on to see if they still fit (hence the "Decide later" box). The reason you want to avoid these kinds of diversions is that it is easy to go astray in the process of organizing.

It might even be helpful for you to set a timer so that you know that you're working against the clock. When the timer dings, you're done for the day, no matter how much work there is still left to do. When your session is complete, don't forget to celebrate your accomplishment in some way—shoot some photos, have a cookie, a nap, or a bath—whatever it takes to make you feel great about what you've done.

Your Road Map

If you're heading into unfamiliar terrain, you're going to need a road map. Before you begin putting items back into that closet you just cleaned out, determine what specific purpose the newly organized closet will have—will it store your everyday wardrobe, your coats, your linens? Be sure that your plans for each closet are directly related to location—you want your possessions to be as close as possible to the area where they will be used so that pickup is not a chore. How should you start? Begin by deciding which items taken out of the unorganized closet actually belong there and which items should be stored elsewhere. Next, eliminate or discard anything that's damaged, outdated, not your style, or the wrong size.

Now that you've discarded what you no longer need from your closets, consider whether you'll eventually replace those items. For example, if you've discarded work clothes that are no longer in style or that no longer fit, will you buy new ones in the near future to replace them? If so, make sure you allocate room in your closet for these new purchases. The idea with closet organization is not to come up with every smart storage solution you can, but to let go of items so that you have some empty closet space. This way, as your needs grow, your closets will "expand" to incorporate new items instead of becoming cluttered and unusable.

Watch Out!

Remember that before donating worn pants, skirts, coats, handbags, and wallets, you should check every pocket and zipper compartment to make sure each one is completely empty. A couple of years ago, a British man discovered he was out of luck when he accidentally left the equivalent of more than $2,000 in the pocket of a donated jacket.

Although you're seeking to pare down, you'll still want to think in terms of efficient storage. Take some time to evaluate the contents of your closet. What is the best way to actually store your belongings?

Hanging On

You want to make sure that you put a storage system in place. But first, make sure you've got adequate lighting. If you can't see it, you won't wear it. No need to call in a professional electrician. Go to your local hardware store and buy an easy-to-install battery-operated closet light. Be sure to give your closet a thorough cleaning, too. Wet-mop floors and wipe down shelves. Dirt and dust balls work their way in and wind up on your clothes. Unknowingly, you may be aggravating your allergies by stopping housecleaning at your closet door.

Older homes are notorious for having small closets. In fact, some oldies-but-goodies have none at all. Before the late nineteenth century, cupboards, cabinets, and stand-alone wardrobes kept belongings in check. Then again, most people had relatively few possessions, especially compared to their twenty-first-century counterparts.

Sometimes older homes lack closets by design. New owners of pre-war homes have been known to take out the lowly closets altogether in order to get more floor space out of small master bedrooms. In the old days, armoires were freestanding closets of choice. You can still eke out prime acreage in a narrow closet. Take a good look at its depth. Is there room to have one rod up front and a second rod behind for the clothes you don't wear as often? Perhaps it's the place for storing off-season gear.

The Bottom Line

It wasn't until around the 1850s that people started using hangers to store clothing in stand-alone wardrobes and closets. Before that, clothing either hung on hooks or lay flat in trunks.

The truth is that the standard closet design of any size, with just a single rod and a shelf above it, utilizes space very inefficiently. If you're willing to invest $2,000–$4,000, you may want to investigate a custom closet system, especially if you're planning to stay in your home for the foreseeable future.

Considering Closet Organizers

Closet organizers and specialized hangers are inexpensive items that can improve the functionality of your closets. Several types of organizers fit easily into any closet. To find out what organizers will work best for you, ask yourself the following questions:

1. Based on the appearance and organization of your closet now, what can you change to make it more organized and functional?

2. Is the space currently being used efficiently?

3. Is there enough room to install drawers and/or cabinets with doors that open and close?

4. Do you need more shelf space, hanging space, and/or drawers in the closet? If so, how will you utilize this space?

5. Can you get by using specialty hangers as opposed to doing construction and installing a customized closet organizer?

6. Is the floor space and door space being utilized right now, or are shoes and other items stored inefficiently?

To determine how much room you have for closet organizers (discussed in the following section), carefully measure the empty closet. Round each measurement to an eighth of an inch, taking the time to be as accurate as possible. Be sure to write the measurements down as you take them, and check your work twice.

When measuring a reach-in closet, determine the width of the closet by measuring the inside space between the two sidewalls, determine the height by measuring from the floor to the ceiling, and determine the depth by measuring the distance between the inside surface of the face wall or door and the back wall.

To measure a walk-in closet, measure the width of each wall, determine the closet's height by measuring from floor to ceiling, determine the width of the doorway by measuring the distance from frame to frame, and measure the height of the doorway, too.

General Organizers

Visit any linen superstore or check out almost any catalog or web-site that features closet organizational products and you'll find a wide selection of closet organizers. These component-based storage systems allow you to customize the inside of your closets without the high cost of hiring a professional to do it. After you've measured your available closet space and know exactly what you want to store in your closet, you can design a closet-storage system by mixing and matching modules.

Shelves and Shelf Dividers

Shelves provide you with a place to put all of the things that would otherwise go on the floor or in a dresser drawer. Preassembled stackable shelves are one option. They're available in a variety of sizes and can be customized to fit the dimensions of your closet. You can purchase closet shelving at most home-improvement or hardware stores.

Shelf dividers separate your shelf into small sections that you can use for a stack of sweaters or a stash of purses, without having them tumble over or get creased or scratched. Keep in mind, however, that it can be a bit of a headache to keep these items orderly. If you've ever grabbed a neatly folded sweater from the bottom of similar stack at a retail store, you know how easily these systems disintegrate into chaos. Other divider systems organize socks, hosiery, jewelry, and folded linens.

Clothes Hangers

When organizing any clothing closet, you want to purchase a variety of clothes hangers. Large wooden hangers are ideal for heavy clothes such as coats. They will also help these items retain their shape. Before you decide which types of hangers are best for you, purge all bent and out-of-shape metal hangers.

Suit hangers are designed with a special pant rod so that the single hanger neatly holds both pants and a jacket. Cedar hangers absorb moisture and discourage pests (such as moths) from damaging your clothing. Collapsible, multitiered hangers save space by allowing you to hang multiple garments in one small area.

Tie and Belt Racks

Although ties and belts are loose items, you can still organize and display them in your closet. Special holders or storage tacks for neckties and belts can be attached to a closet wall or door, or in some cases can be hung from the closet's rod. Some racks also slide out when you need them and tuck away when you don't. Be sure to store tie racks close to dress shirts so that coordinating outfits is easy. Pegs with nubbed tips keep ties in place and prevent wrinkling.

Shoe-Ins

Shoes are the most problematic part of our wardrobe, at least from a neat freak's perspective. On average, women own something like thirty pairs of shoes, and most aren't likely to forsake their mules, pumps, sandals, and loafers for any extra closet space. Even when it comes to athletic footwear, we've got one set for tennis, another for walking, a third for jogging. Banish the thought of an all-purpose multisport sneaker, even for the most nominal of exercisers.

The answer isn't a high pile of shoes in their branded shoe boxes, even if the boxes are stacked neat as a pin. Unless you've got Superman's X-ray vision, it's a good bet you don't even know what's in each box. Instead of ready-to-wear, you've got a mountain of forget-to-wear.

If you fancy yourself the arts-and-crafts type, you can snap a picture of the shoes and tape it to the outside of the box for identification, but let's face it. That kind of über-organization takes ongoing commitment. Nice to think about, but who's got the time? Purchase plastic see-through boxes, instead. There's no guessing involved. And keep those piles of shoe boxes low. Otherwise, reaching for a pair way down on the bottom will set off an avalanche. Can the inside of your closet door or a section of interior wall accommodate a hanging shoe organizer? It's a great way to keep footwear orderly, accessible—and in pairs. How many times have you found yourself stumbling around for a renegade shoe that fell somewhere deep in the back of the closet floor?

The Bottom Line

Shoes will look good and feel good if you keep them in tip-top shape. Always use a shoehorn to protect the integrity of the heels. Shoe trees will help hold the shape and can prolong their life; cedar trees will absorb moisture. Allow shoes to breath between wearings; try not to dress in the same pair on consecutive days.

Revolving shoe carousels take up minimal floor space, though you'll need to clear about three feet of height for an eighteen-pair revolving system. Boots are always a bit clumsier to manage. Boot trees will help them hold their shape better, keeping them upright and more neatly aligned. Clear boot boxes are a better idea if your boot collection numbers more than a few.

Coats

Coats are tough to part with. They last years, but before you know it, you've got an accumulation for every occasion. There's the special dress-up coat for celebrations, the everyday jacket, and the weatherproof utility number for nor'easters. Pare down and donate the ones you haven't worn in a while. Instead of storing gloves in coat pockets, scarves around the hangers, and hats who knows where, use the vertical space above the rod. Mesh or clear bins are perfect ways to keep accessories accounted for and dust-free. You can also nail small baskets to the inside of the closet door and allocate one basket to each family member's accessories. Install a few hooks for grab-and-go items like umbrellas, purses, knapsacks, and gym bags.

An Organized Inquiry

Why is cold storage recommended for leather coats? Heat and humidity can dry out the oils in furs and leathers. Professional cold storage in temperature-controlled vaults during the warmer months will increase the life span of your leather and maintain its peak condition.

It's likely that coats are not the only things in your coat closet. In many homes, coat closets are a catchall for a growing collection of shopping bags, wrapping paper rolls, and cleaning appliances. You're better off not jamming the closet to the gills. Coats need to breathe, and you need to see exactly what's in there. If you're going to turn it into a multipurpose closet, create zones.

Of course, it's not realistic to think that your closet will always stay perfect—and they don't need to. But if you did a good job setting up a system of organization, then you should find that your closets are more user-friendly than they were before. Keeping things neat should take less effort now. If you find kinks in your system along the way, feel free to make adjustments. Change labels on containers, reorganize clothing or shoes, and do whatever it takes to find what works for you. You'll get it right in time.

Chapter 11
Hide Your Dirty Laundry

MANY PEOPLE THINK OF LAUNDRY AS A CHORE that is to be avoided at all costs. But if you can organize your laundry room in a way that is visually appealing and functional, laundry day doesn't have to cause groans. This chapter has tips for organizing your laundry area and simplifying the laundering process, as well as advice about how to get tough stains out of clothing.

Neglected Laundry

Life is often such a whirlwind that it can be a challenge to slow down and give laundry the attention it deserves. And when we're unable to be attentive to each stage of the process, we're more likely to suffer from laundry chaos. The FlyLady compares laundry to a neglected child that turns up everywhere: "You can catch it hanging out in unsavory places: mildewed in hampers; stinky and soured in washers for days; cold and wrinkled in dryers; wadded up in baskets stashed beside beds; or folded nice and neat and left abandoned in the laundry room."

Doing the laundry doesn't have to be burdensome, though. Nor does it need to consume the entire day. There are things that you can do to make this task feel more pleasant. First of all, think about the space where you do laundry. If you are lucky enough to have your own washer and dryer, there are ways that you can arrange the space to increase your efficiency. The next section outlines a few important ideas related to your laundry area.

Organizing Your Laundry Area

Wherever you locate your washer and dryer, you can probably better organize the area of your home that's dedicated to laundry. In a perfect world, a laundry area would offer the following:

- Ample space for a full-sized washer and dryer (remember to leave at least a few inches between each of these appliances and the nearby walls)

- Shelving or cabinets to store detergents and fabric softeners (the room will look less cluttered if you utilize cabinets with doors, so items can be stored out of sight)

- Space for keeping laundry baskets or hampers of dirty clothing

- An area for ironing, steaming, and folding clean clothes

- An area to hang wet clothing that needs to be line-dried

- Storage for hangers and/or a place to hang garments

- A sink for hand-washing garments

- A wastebasket

- A television, radio, and/or telephone with a speaker option to occupy your mind while you fold and iron

- Ample lighting, so you can separate different-colored clothing, identify badly stained garments for special treatment, and read the handling instructions printed on the small labels of some garments

- Temperature control, because if the laundry area gets too cold (especially in a basement), the water pipes could freeze; if the room is too hot, it will be unbearable to work in the room

Unless you live in a large house or have allocated a section of your basement to accommodate all of the above-listed needs for space, chances are you'll have to improvise. Most people do, anyway. Perhaps you want to set up a laundry line outside (if your local climate is appropriate for this), or you may even want to install a retractable line above your bathtub.

One of the most important things to keep in mind when organizing your laundry area is that you want your detergents and fabric softener to be within arm's reach of the washer and dryer. Ideally, the flooring beneath your washer and dryer will be waterproof, should a flood occur. You'll also want to place an overflow container under the washer to prevent water from escaping the immediate area, should the washer overflow or leak.

Hampers

While some people have large rooms devoted to laundry, others make do with a small alcove in the bathroom or a closet. For those who must pack a lot of laundry into a small space, it is critical to think of ways to simplify the space so that everything you need is stored in a way that is compact, efficient, and attractive.

If your laundry room is in a busy part of the house—or in a hallway, bathroom, or alcove—you might want to invest in a hamper that will conceal your dirty laundry. If you purchase a triple hamper—with a bin for white, light colors and dark ones—then you can simplify your life by sorting the items before they go into the hamper.

Ironing Boards

Although many people like to have a full-sized ironing board, it can take up a lot of space and be a hassle to set up and take down if you do not have a stand-alone laundry room. If your laundry space is compact, you might purchase an ironing board that comes in its own cabinet, can fold out when needed, and then be neatly concealed.

Consider Cabinets

Another great addition to any laundry space is some cabinetry above the washer and dryer. This will allow you to store your detergent and laundry supplies out of sight, and will also afford you some useful storage for linens, towels, and other items. If the cabinetry is directly above your washer and dryer, then extra blankets, sheets and towels can simply be folded there and tucked directly into these cabinets. Be sure that there is a decent gap—at least two feet—between your appliances and the cabinets so that you have easy access to top loading machines and so that the contents of your cabinets are not exposed to too much heat or humidity.

Another benefit of cabinets—especially when a laundry area is part of another room or located in a hallway or closet—is that cabinetry can allow for a cohesive look in an area that might otherwise look thrown together. Cabinetry can distinguish the space that is used for laundry in a way that is both decorative and functional.

Flat Surfaces

Now that laundry rooms are so often small and tucked away, it can sometimes be a challenge to find a flat surface for folding clothes. If you can integrate a secondhand table or a countertop into your laundry area, this will facilitate the folding process. Think in terms of comfort as well—if you think that you'll want to sit while folding, put a comfortable chair beside the table. Make sure that you have a radio or television nearby as well, to decrease the monotony of folding your clothes.

You'll also want to be aware of lighting in this area—you'll enjoy being in there if it is adequate but not overbearing. Few people want to work happily under the glare of fluorescents. Remember that lighting can set the mood of a room, and ideally, your laundry area will be inviting and warm so that you'll actually want to spend time there. Changing the lighting doesn't have to cost much, either. Sometimes the simple addition of a floor lamp that glows instead of glares can transform the feel of the room.

Bring In Some Beauty

Who said that a laundry area has to be ugly? Especially if your laundry area is in the basement or another part of your home that does not receive much natural light, consider painting the walls a cheering color. Hang artwork or photographs that you enjoy looking at near your washer and dryer. These small touches can increase the human element of a space that is more typically dominated by machines.

Although cabinets can be functional and beautiful, they may be out of your price range. If this is the case, you can use baskets instead. A few square baskets on a shelf above the washer and dryer can be useful for keeping detergents and fabric softeners in order, and they can also add some texture and visual appeal to the area.

Everyone develops a personalized system for doing laundry. The layout and design of your laundry facilities should complement your work habits in order to make this task as stress-free and easy as possible.

Simplifying the Process

When was the last time you did several loads of laundry, wound up with missing socks, had the dye from a new pair of jeans run all over your other clothes, and then ended up with a wrinkled mess after everything came out of the dryer? Everyone has had these laundry nightmares happen, but virtually all laundry disasters and mishaps can be avoided by taking an organized approach to cleaning your clothes.

Too Much Laundry?

While working out how to best do the laundry, think about the amount of laundry you do every week. Is there any way that you can decrease your load? Do you sometimes wash clothing that isn't really dirty or linens that could be used for a few more days?

In *Simplify Your Life*, Elaine St. James suggests that while automatic washers and dryers greatly simplify the process of laundering clothing, modern Americans may be spending just as much time doing laundry as they were fifty years ago. While modern conveniences have the potential to ease our backs and make the work less labor intensive, they may not actually be reducing the amount of time we spend actually laundering our clothes.

How could this be? Because of the great ease with which clothing can be washed, many people wash their clothes far too frequently. The frenzied pace of contemporary life can sometimes cause the illusion that it is actually easier to toss a once-worn shirt into the hamper than it is to take a moment and neatly fold the shirt and place it back in a drawer or closet. The contemporary obsession with cleanliness may also add to the myth that a shirt or pants worn once is somehow "contaminated" and must be washed immediately.

Elaine St. James, however, points out that this attitude is a great departure from the practices fifty years ago, when the effort involved in laundry dictated that all family members be more careful about clothes. She writes, "In the old days, for example, Grandpa would put on a clean shirt on Monday and after wearing it carefully through the week, it would go into the clothes hamper for Grandma to take care of on wash day. Now, we think nothing of wearing two or three shirts a day—one for exercise, one for work, one for casual wear—and casually throwing them into the laundry."

The problem with clothing also extends to linens, according to St. James. Many people actually use a fresh towel and washcloth every single day, but this luxury can be costly in the long run. Not only does running the washer use water and energy, but it requires the vigilant efforts of a laundress. If each member of the family can reduce the amount of clothing and linens placed in the hamper each week, then the effort involved in laundering can be greatly reduced.

Word to the Wise

Elaine St. James urges her readers to try to limit the amount of time spent doing laundry to just one load per person per week. If family members know that only so much can be cleaned, they are likely to be more discriminating about what gets tossed into the hamper, easing the burden of the primary laundry caretaker.

A Wardrobe Malfunction?

If you find that you consistently don't want to do laundry, try to get to the heart of the problem. Many times, resistance to doing laundry is related to problems in other parts of the house. If you've had a chance to decrease the amount of clothing in your closets and drawers, for example, you might find that you feel better equipped to do your laundry. If the drawers and closets feel overwhelming, you might be inclined to procrastinate on the final step of putting laundry away.

If this is your situation, take a break from organizing your laundry area and head back to the bedroom. Try to purge items out of a few drawers and see if a little extra space makes a difference in how you feel about putting clothing away. Drawers and closets that are packed too full are not only confusing to navigate early in the morning when you're trying to get ready for work, they also tend to leave clothes looking wrinkly and forgotten.

If you feel a sense of despair related to the idea of neatly folding your clothes, it might be related to the thought that no matter how gingerly you care for your clothes in the laundry area, they are still bound to get all wrinkled as soon as they hit the drawers. Conquer this defeating feeling by tackling the drawers and closets that are the root of the problem.

Think "Laundry Day" While Shopping

Another way to simplify your laundry is to resist impulse purchases. When shopping for clothes, don't just consider the aesthetic appeal of an item. Think also about the effort involved in cleaning it. Elaine St. James believes that life can be greatly simplified if you refuse to purchase clothing that needs to be dry-cleaned.

In certain professions, a dry-clean-only suit may be required, but for those who have the opportunity to dress more casually, eliminating dry-clean-only items from a wardrobe can reduce the hassle and cost of maintaining your clothes.

St. James also encourages people to simplify their lives by purchasing clothing that can be mixed and matched so that you don't always have to be laundering or searching for that one pair of pants that matches that one shirt. If you're really serious about simplifying your life (and you don't mind a little monotony in your wardrobe), purchase multiple pieces that are similar or the same. If you find a pair of argyle socks that you love, for example, buy four pairs so you don't have to waste precious time hunting down that one lone sock.

In *Simplify Your Life,* St. James has suggestions for women to help build a simple wardrobe. She has taken the principles of male wardrobes and adapted them to feminine standards:

- Pick a simple, classic style that looks good on you and then stick with it. Forever.

- Build combinations of outfits that work as a uniform: two or three jackets of the same or similar style but in different, muted shades, with two or three sets of the same or similarly styled skirts and/ or slacks in different muted shades, and a few coordinating shirts, blouses, and tops. Each item should go with every other item.

- Remember that men, for the most part, don't wear jewelry, don't carry purses, and wear only one heel height.

These suggestions may feel a little austere, especially if you are a person who loves color and variety. You can adapt the basic concept, however, to any fashion sensibility. These are not hard and fast rules, but simply one path toward creating a simpler wardrobe, which will help you declutter you life—and your laundry room!

Putting Clothes Away

Putting clothes away can be a hassle, but recently, professional home organizers have begun to advocate an interesting approach to the task. Instead of separating your socks, slacks, and shirts into neat little piles, they advise assembling outfits and then storing entire outfits on hangers or in your drawers. This small step can add ease to your mornings, because you no longer have to look for the skirt that goes with a particular shirt. This approach is also very helpful for children, because sometimes assembling outfits that actually match can be a challenge for them. But if you assemble outfits for them and place similar items together in their drawers, your children will be able to feel independent when they "pick" their own outfit, without actually exercising the kind of independence that will make you cringe when they come out of their rooms.

Like every room in the house, the laundry area is full of challenges, but these challenges can become opportunities. As you become more attuned to bringing order, harmony, and functionality to this part of your life, you might find that the dread associated with doing laundry will decrease. Victoria Moran says that we often dislike monotonous tasks such as cleaning or laundry simply because we feel that they are mindless and perhaps "beneath us." But these concrete tasks are a very real way to care for those who surround us.

After you have rearranged and decorated your laundry area to make it more efficient and appealing, you might find the groans come less often.

Chapter 12
Air Out Your Attic

THE ATTIC TRADITIONALLY HOUSES LONG-FORGOTTEN ITEMS and, more often than not, items better left forgotten. As a result, all that valuable space winds up becoming a holding tank for stuff that might be more appropriately housed at the curb—for trash pickup the next morning. This chapter gives you ideas on reclaiming, rethinking, and reorganizing your attic in ways that use every surface.

States of Disgrace

People should grow old gracefully. The stuff in your attic shouldn't. We allow the pointless mess to fester through sheer inertia. It's so much easier to stow it than to unload it. In fact, the only time most people ever really get a clear picture of what's under their roof is when it's time for them to move.

Let's face it. In our continuing quest for more storage space, the attic is probably the most off-putting place of all, with its creaky floorboards, spider-web décor, and dark, creepy corners. There's practically an entire genre of Hollywood movies dedicated to ghouls-in-the-attic, bodies-in-the-attic, voices-from-the-attic terror.

It's not only an inhospitable environment, it's a harsh one, too. For homes without tree cover, the sun's ultraviolet rays beat down and play havoc with the thermostat levels. And for homes that do have the benefit of ray-blocking branches, there's the potential problem of moss and algae developing around the puddles of fallen leaves.

Newer homes might often be blessed with spacious walk-in closets, but at the same time they're notoriously lacking when it comes to attic space. Many have nothing but a crawl space. Up until a half century ago, homes were smaller, but large attics were the norm. Grandma's attic had lots of headroom, giving her ample space to move around her steamer trunks of stored treasures. But then home-builders began using stronger and less expensive trusses instead of rafters to support the roof. The construction method lowered the roof pitch and, ultimately, cut down on storage opportunities.

The Bottom Line

There are several different types of attic configurations. At one end of the spectrum are limited crawl spaces. At the other are full attics that offer full headroom and can easily be converted into usable living space. If converting the space is under consideration, contact your local housing authority or town government before you make any investments. Many municipalities have strict requirements that may even include installing an indoor sprinkler system.

If you've got a hole-in-the-ceiling kind of attic that's accessible through a hatch, you have a legitimate reason for attic clutter. Lack of access makes it difficult, not to mention precarious, to move belongings up and down, in and out. Then there's the problem of maneuverability. Steeply sloping attic walls make moving around once you're inside a thorny, back-taxing effort.

There's another reason why attics are often the *least* organized area of the household: because you can get away with it. When was the last time a guest paid a visit to your lofty real estate? Exactly. As a result, when you go looking for something in the attic, you know you're in for a Lewis and Clark–caliber expedition. And chances are you will come away from the experience a lot less successful than they were.

Yes, while there is a long list of reasons that make attic storage particularly challenging, it doesn't mean you've got carte blanche to keep a bad system going. Nor does it mean you need to throw up your arms and surrender. It's not a question of abandoning the attic space as much as it is bowing to its limitations.

Consider Access

You can't organize your attic if you can't get into it, right? Making your attic more accessible ups the chances that you'll actually go into, use, and organize it.

If you'll be using the attic as a storage area and will need to gain access to this space often, you might want to replace the basic access-panel entrance (which you may need a ladder to get to) with a pull-down staircase. Also, install a light switch or light pull-string near the entrance to the attic. You don't want to be climbing around in the dark. For information on pull-down staircases, visit any hardware or home-improvement store. You can also point your web browser to the Louisville Ladder website (*www.ladderpros.com*) and click on Products—Attic Ladders.

Word to the Wise

If reaching your attic means getting a stepladder from the basement and hauling it upstairs, chances are you're not making good use of the space. Instead, install a permanent wood or aluminum pull-down ladder. It's a do-it-yourself project that will make attic access easier and, more important, safer.

Consider weather when organizing your attic. In other words, know that you'll be storing your items in a non–climate-controlled environment (with potential hazards such as water, mildew, mold, insects, and/or rodents), and take the appropriate precautions. Airtight plastic storage containers are useful and economical—make sure they're clear so that you can see the contents, but don't forget to label them as well.

Thinking Outside the Carton

It helps to keep a simple premise in mind: What goes up must come down. There really shouldn't be such a thing as permanent storage in your house in the first place. It's a sign your storage system has broken down. Permanent storage is dead storage. Few people can afford the luxury of giving over space without a fight when the rest of their living quarters has them feeling crowded in. If you're stowing something under the rafters and then simply forgetting about it, it's a good bet you didn't really need it in the first place.

So, throughout the attic-organization process, be critical about the items stored there. You might want to ask yourself if the items up there are even needed—if you haven't thought about them for years, they might not be important enough to keep.

Here is a list of items that every home can do without:

- Old tools that don't work

- Luggage that is broken or cumbersome to use (especially if you've updated your luggage)

- Mildewed or damaged furniture

- College textbooks (in some cases, these could be useful, but in most fields the material becomes quickly obsolete)

- Old mattresses that are just collecting dust

- Appliances that no longer work or are rarely used

- Cassette tapes and VHS tapes if you only use a DVD/CD player

Be attentive to the things around you that are taking up precious space. Although it can be painful to let certain items go, it is visually thrilling to see your home with less clutter. The FlyLady says that decluttering allows your home to breathe. Keep in mind that by decluttering you may be giving your home a great gift—the gift of fresh life.

That's not to say that attic storage doesn't have a place in your home organizational scheme. Reserve the attic for items used infrequently, as long as they can stand up to the potential of extreme hot and cold temperature swings. In many cases, the attic is a sound storage option for the same types of items you house in your basement, such as luggage, holiday decorations, and seasonal clothing. But leave woolen fabrics downstairs. They're like a banquet to pests. Soiled clothes and fabrics are especially attractive to vermin, so make sure you clean all items before stowing. Use canvas garment bags for clothes, and include pest control protection material, such as cedar chips.

The attic is also a good place for old files that you don't need instant access to but are still required to keep, such as tax returns, closing documents, and mortgage paperwork. Keep paperwork in a heavy-duty plastic or fireproof metal cabinet.

If you store rugs in the attic, clean them first. Then roll them tightly, secure with rope, and label.

An Organized Inquiry

What does the R-value of insulation refer to? The R-value is a measure that indicates how well insulation resists heat flow. The higher the R-value, the better the insulation. Insulation should be added in any area that separates a heated space from an unheated space.

In contrast to basement environments, attics tend to be dry as long as there's good insulation and ventilation. On the other hand, if an attic hasn't been properly prepped for storage use, extreme heat and high moisture conditions can be detrimental to certain items. One forward-thinking shopper bought all of her holiday cards the day after Christmas at half price and put them in the attic for safekeeping. But when she retrieved them the following December, she discovered the heat caused the glue on her envelopes to seal shut. So much for her "sale."

Other attic storage no-no's are cosmetics and food, along with most types of media like photographs, videotapes, film, and slides. They just won't hold up well under the punishing conditions.

Watch Out!

Check the labels of all items before storing in the attic. Make sure that none of the items have a label warning: "Keep away from heat or flame." You might be surprised what liquids are combustible. Summer heat could create a hazardous situation.

Be sure your attic can meet the weight demands of whatever you have stored there. The last thing you want to create is a situation in which the ceiling below the floorboards is compromised.

Empty the Attic

As difficult as the thought may be, to undertake a thorough job, you've got to roll up your sleeves and find out what's there, which means emptying out the attic contents. That's right—every last carton, trunk, and cabinet. Now before you toss this book down and run, think about the upside. You'll doubtless come across items you can discard, which will allow you to relocate things from other overcrowded parts of your home. You'll probably discover some sentimental treasures, too, so get ready to be hit with a big fat wave of nostalgia. Your wedding dress, high school yearbook, maybe even your grade-school diary might just be squirreled away up there somewhere in cartons unknown. Perhaps you'll even find some investment-grade treasures. One woman had a Depression glass collection in her attic for ages. When she first stored it up there, Depression glass was considered inexpensive, run-of-the-mill dinnerware: nothing special and, certainly, of no real value. When she unwrapped it from the yellowed newspapers decades later, it had become a sought-after antique.

Word to the Wise

A whole-house attic exhaust fan works wonders to minimize extreme temperature swings and to reduce moisture levels. The exhaust fan draws hot air out of your attic and replaces it with the cooler outside air. A stable environment will add to the longevity of your stored goods.

If you access your attic via a ladder, enlist the assistance of one or two people who can take items from you without your having to negotiate an armload of stuff up and down the steps. It's a safety precaution that'll be kinder on your back and arms, too, and move the process along.

Warehousing items for friends, grown children, or other family members? Well, this is as good a time as any to remind them about their belongings and invite them to join you in the reorganizing process. Chances are they've probably forgotten about the items altogether. If you're really serious about downsizing your attic clutter, you might even want to give them an "expiration date" to take their items out of your home by—politely, of course! Set up a nearby staging area by making room for your four piles:

- **Trash:** For large items, you may need to schedule a special trash pickup with your local municipality.

- **Donation:** Before you make a call to a charitable agency, make sure your contributions are still in good condition and working order. They don't want junk any more than you do.

- **Relocate:** You may actually find a few things deserving of a second chance or—eureka!—something you've been trying to track down forever.

- **Save:** Back to long-term storage for these babies, but review them carefully to make sure your attic is, indeed, the best place for them.

Lay down a tarp or old sheet before you get going, since you're likely to kick up a lot of dust. Some people even wear inexpensive dust masks, available at any hardware store.

When taking inventory, don't just open a box, sneak a quick peek, and seal it up again. Really go through your things in detail. If you need a nudge to help you add items onto the discard pile, just think about climbing back up into the attic with those containers again. That should do the trick. The key is to be honest with yourself about what you need and what you can really live without. Don't guilt trip yourself into keeping items given as gifts that you have no use for now or in the future.

Watch Out!

Squirrels can be unwelcome guests in your attic. Take pre-emptive measures before they take shelter. Cut down overhanging tree branches that might make it easier for them to reach your attic. Look for possible entry holes and seal them up. Install vent covers, since attic vents are also common entry points.

Make the Best Use of Your Space

Begin organizing your attic by determining how you plan to utilize this space. Decide what you want to store in your attic, and then measure the attic space carefully and make sure it's suitable for your needs. Prepare your attic for its intended purpose, eliminating potential hazards.

Using a pad of paper and your measurements, draw a rough layout of the area and determine how and where you'll be storing your various belongings. Figure out whether you'll first need to install additional shelving, lighting, flooring, or anything else to make your attic space more usable.

After you've had a chance to remove the clutter from your attic, give the space a good cleaning. This cleaning is not only useful for your sense of well-being, but it can also lead to important information. Perhaps your roof has a leak that you hadn't known about. A good cleaning can reveal water spots, squirrels' nests, and all sorts of hidden problems. After the area is cleaned out, begin arranging the items you're storing in the attic. Put items you won't need often in places where they're less readily available. As you arrange boxes and other items in the attic, make sure air vents are unobstructed. Also, if there is a ventilation fan in the attic, make sure your items are kept away from it.

Start the Process

Now that your attic is all cleaned up, it's time to begin the organization process. As you start, remember that attics, like all good storage areas of your home, need zones of their own. Determine what categories you're working with and then assign areas accordingly. You may have set areas for the following:

- Housewares

- Holiday decorations

- Memorabilia

- Books

- Furniture

- Exercise equipment

- Toys and games

- Electronics

If different individuals store their possessions in your attic, carve out a section for each one.

Attics aren't the kind of places you want to linger a minute longer than necessary. Move it in or move it out. Period. When you put similar items together, you make things much easier to find. And when it's time to return them, you'll already know just where to go. It's like having a road map. We all know that rummaging through an attic in extreme heat or cold isn't any fun. As a matter of fact, when scheduling your plan of attack, tackle attic organization during a time of the year when room temperatures are most comfortable. No matter how much enthusiasm you might muster for the task or how much you psych yourself up for it, you won't get far if the thermometer is in single—or triple—digits.

Consider creating a simple inventory map for your attic. It'll help you locate your stored items in a jiffy. Even if you know exactly where things are, others in your household might not. Tack the map up near the attic entrance or in some other well-lit, easy-to-find location.

It's Worth It!

Although tackling your attic can be a daunting task, there are many hidden rewards to this kind of project. You may even be able to enlarge your home, without the cost of an addition. You'll also regain access to those things that you need and love.

And, if you are able to remove clutter and donate it to charity, you'll have the opportunity to be socially and ecologically responsible. Instead of all that stuff wasting away in the dark, cobwebby corners of your basement and attic, at least some of these items could be put to use by those who need them, and others could be recycled into something useful for others to enjoy. Meanwhile, you'll have the opportunity to live in less cluttered, more streamlined space. As Leonardo da Vinci wrote, "Simplicity is the ultimate sophistication."

Chapter 13

Better Your Basement

THE BASEMENT MAY JUST BE THE MOST UNSTRUCTURED, do-what-you-will-with-it room in the house. It can be the family center, gym, hobby room, office, or party place. It could be all of the above. It could also be the dark dungeon you dread to enter. Whatever the case, finished or unfinished, chances are it's one of your home's prime storage areas.

You might often be tempted to think "Out of sight, out of mind"—yet all that clutter stored below can weigh on you. It can also be a fire hazard as well as a haven for unwanted pests. This chapter explores ways to make the best use of that utilitarian space with a host of surefire ways to keep the boxes and junk at bay.

Down in the Dumps

When people talk about being down in the dumps, they could be referring to their basements, also known as the dumping ground. If you've got a case of subterranean blues, it could be because you've taken an out-of-sight, out-of-mind approach to clearing out the clutter. You move stuff down, but never out. And out—by the curb, that is—is probably where a lot of it belongs. Some of the tidiest homes have the untidiest underbellies lurking beneath their floorboards. Like closets, basements are an easy place to let things get out of hand. Company's coming, so downstairs the clutter goes. The trouble is, it never comes back up to be returned to its proper places. The clutter just builds and builds and builds. . . .

Word to the Wise

Make it easy to part with your outgrown or rarely worn clothes. Leave a "charity" bag right by your laundry area. That way when an unwanted item comes out of the washer or dryer, it goes right into the bag, making it one step closer to finding a more deserving home. When the bag's full, it's time to call your favorite charity for a pickup.

Do any of these scenarios describe the situation in your basement?

- You moved into your new home, stored some cartons down there to get them out of the way "for the time being," and then—oops!— never looked back.

- Your son, sister, cousin, or uncle left some items down there for safekeeping—years ago. Now the area's become a multigenerational chest, not of treasures but of outgrown, worn-out, and long-forgotten belongings.

- Your basement has become the land of backups. You've got your pre-Y2K computer, first-generation scanner, sparks-ridden toaster oven, and dishes that no longer match your kitchen décor packed down there—just in case you ever need them.

- You never met an empty carton you didn't like, or least one you didn't want to hold on to. After all, you never know when you'll need to crate up that bulky piece of electronics or appliance again . . . right?

- Your basement is a tangled heap of Valentine's Day, Easter, Independence Day, Halloween, or Christmas decorations. You can't get up the
  energy to organize any of it, let alone actually put them on display.

And that's assuming you even know what's down there at all. More
often than not, items are packed in newspaper and then socked away
in unmarked boxes. Or worse. One unfortunate homeowner put out an
SOS after a dreadful discovery. The home she moved into had an old,
unplugged freezer in the basement. She assumed the freezer was empty
and never bothered to open it. When it was time to install a new furnace,
the old unit had to be moved. It was only then that the hapless homeowner opened the freezer for the very first time to discover it was filled
with eight-year-old rotted meat. What will you unearth in your basement?
Isn't it time you took a good look at what you've got down there?

More than the clutter that plagues any other room in the house, basement clutter can go on for years before you finally reach the "I've had it"
stage. In fact, it can go for decades if you live in one place long enough.
Even when people get up the motivation to reorganize their homes, the
basement is the place most of them save for last when it comes to a
streamlining overhaul. The turning point often comes when it's time to
move elsewhere or when you start thinking about reworking the space for
another use, such as converting it into a family room or home gym. Then
you're left to face the music. Don't wait. Now's the time to give your dead
storage a little CPR and let the space work to your advantage.

The Bottom Line

Among the different types of basements, poured concrete is the most
popular. Other types are masonry walls that are made out of blocks and
sealed to prevent seepage and precast panel basements in which concrete
panels are poured at the factory, transported to the site, and then lifted
into place with a crane.

Get Everyone Involved

Before you start to panic, take a deep breath and remind yourself that you don't have to organize these areas in a single afternoon—nor should you take on this task all by yourself. Julie Morgenstern writes that basements should be family projects if you want to enjoy them over the long haul. Everyone should have something invested in keeping that area in order. Prior to beginning to organize the basement, she suggests that you have a family meeting so that each member can consider what he might gain through a more organized basement or attic.

The chaos in the attic or basement could be preventing your family from enjoying the space to the fullest. Not only does chaos make it harder to retrieve items when you need them, it can also prevent your family from spreading into these parts of the house. Could your basement or attic provide a play room for small children or an entertainment area for older ones? If so, talk that up! You're likely to get more cooperation from your children if they know that there is something in this project for them.

Getting Started

The first thing you need to do is to give yourself some elbow room to work. Scan the room and set your priorities on eliminating the most obvious, aisle-jamming items: the old ice skates, the large picture frame with the cracked glass you've been meaning to replace, the ancient air conditioner you trip over at every turn. Moving them to the side to create aisles isn't good enough. Getting rid of things is the name of the game.

The basement is typically reserved for big bulky items. For that reason, when you're ready to start sorting, it often makes sense to relegate those things into piles rather than bother with cartons or trash bags. Let one area be for your keepers. You're likely to find a lot of sentimental favorites down there—photos, stuffed animals, even family heirlooms.

Weeding Out

Depending on the item, you may need to move these to more appropriate public spaces where you can actually enjoy them—but not just yet. If you stop what you're doing to relocate items to other rooms of the house, you'll get distracted from the task at hand and never finish the job.

Clear another section for your giveaways. If you're planning to hold some for, say, a future garage sale, put those items all together in one area and clearly label them so that the only other time you'll need to go through the collection again is the day of the actual sale. Your final pile is for your throwaways. Be sure to get rid of anything that's been damaged by humidity or pests. Now is also the time to dump anything that's obsolete, rusty, or not in working order. Lose the ceiling fan with the broken blade, the dot-matrix printer, and the coffee table with the bum leg. You probably have a few old cans of paint, varnish, and dried-up stucco there, too. Dispose of them, but make sure you do it in accordance with your local regulations. If your throwaways seem intimidatingly large and heavy because you've allowed the situation to degenerate for so long, you might consider hiring a trash removal service like 1-800-GOT-JUNK to do the heavy lifting and haul them out of your house for you.

An Organized Inquiry

What do I do if my basement has a mildew problem? Here are a few tactics you can try to rid the room of the odor. If you've got windows, leave them open to vent the room. Use a dehumidifier, and if there's carpeting, give it a good deep cleaning.

A few words about the keepers. First, don't put anything back in cartons or storage containers without making sure the box is clearly labeled on multiple sides. Clear plastic containers will help take some of the guesswork out of the process, too. Avoid making the boxes too heavy or stacking them too high. If they're too hard to move, you'll be tempted to let them stay where they are for good. Store only the items that intuitively make sense as belonging in your basement. Gardening tools, for instance, are better housed in your garage or shed. Segregate items so that like items are all in one place. Think of it as you would a retail store, keeping all kitchen items together in one spot, sports equipment in another, and so on. The best storage solutions are the most logical ones.

Word to the Wise

When positioning items on shelves, make sure the heaviest bottles, cartons, and cans are on low reinforced shelves, close to the floor. House lighter and more frequently used items on the most accessible shelves—figure somewhere between waist high and eye level.

Keep that retail image going a bit longer as you strategize your organizational goals. Putting items on old baking racks or similar shelving units will help clear the floor space, giving you room to maneuver and the ability to access items easier. Hooks and pegboards will help, too. You can put abandoned furniture back to work down here as makeshift storage holders. Breathe new life into old lockers, pantry units, and bookcases. If you're planning a kitchen remodeling job, think about setting up your old cabinets here.

What shouldn't you keep down in the basement? Well, it depends on the climate conditions. Dampness and sweaty walls are often problems, especially in older homes. And there's always a chance of flooding, so chemicals as well as items of special value should be stored above potential flood levels. If your basement is prone to high humidity or flooding conditions, here are some items you'd be wise to store in other areas of your home:

- Precious mementos
- Books
- Photograph albums
- Artwork
- Letters and cards

On the other hand, the basement is a fine place to store household management items like cleaning products and bulk supplies. Keep nonperishable foods, paper towels, napkins, bath tissue, and light bulbs on shelves or, better yet, in dust-free and pest-proof cabinets. Stack items in a way in which you can easily see what you've got. Then you'll know when it's time to restock. It'll also prevent you from buying extras unnecessarily.

Other items well suited for basement storage are pieces of big, bulky sporting equipment, like camping supplies and ski gear, as well as tools, holiday decorations, and party supplies.

Store luggage here, too. Unless you're a road warrior who's on a plane every week and needs to have your bags always at the ready, there's an advantage to storing your luggage in the basement rather than clogging up a high-trafficked closet. Just keep an eye on those suitcases every once in a while to make sure mold doesn't form due to excess humidity. For space efficiency, nestle smaller suitcases inside the large ones. The area under the stairs is an especially good place to stow luggage, but make sure to keep your bags away from any windows in case there are leaks.

Basements have always been a good place to store wine because of the darkness and their cool temperatures. If you have a collection, store bottles on their sides to prevent the corks from drying out. Also, make sure the bottles are a safe distance away from the furnace, hot water heater, and other heat-producing equipment. Group them by category: reds, whites, dessert wines, and aperitifs.

Watch Out!

Mold spores require moisture to grow and thrive, and areas of the home where there's water buildup from high humidity or flooding are ideal growing conditions. If you've got musty odors or spot clusters of dark specks, both good indications of mold, it's time to take action.

A Good Cleaning

Before you start putting things away in your basement, take the time to give it a thorough cleaning first. The great thing about clearing out the basement is that now that you can see the floors and walls, you can get the dust and spiders out of there. Before you put anything back into the space, make sure that you've cleaned out the cobwebs. Otherwise, even if you've created some order, you'll probably still dread going down to the basement. Who wants to encounter spiders, dust, and grime?

To protect the items to be stored, think about what's required: cardboard boxes, airtight plastic containers, shelves, drawers, coverings (tarps), and so on. You can also store items by hanging them from the basement ceiling.

Next, install the shelving, lighting, or other organizational tools you believe are necessary. After the room is prepared, fill your basement with the items you plan to store there, starting with the largest items first.

As you evaluate your storage plan, answer the following questions:

- Are the items you're storing easy to find and readily accessible?

- Are the items you're storing far enough away from your laundry area or workshop area? Is there a clear path to your working appliances, as well as ample space to work and play?

- If you have children, does your storage area provide any potential hazards? Should certain items be locked up separately?

- Have you protected your belongings against natural disasters and pests (flooding, mildew, mold, insects, and rodents)?

- Are your stored items in the way of your home's hot water heater, furnace, fuse box, washer, dryer, or any other appliances in use within the basement? Are all drains and pipes clear from any obstruction?

If you're storing plastic crates or boxes, stack them up against a wall, making sure they are stable and won't fall. Also, make sure that the labels (describing what's in each box) are facing outward and are easily readable. Place the larger and heavier boxes on the bottom, and the lighter ones above them. Items stored in boxes at the bottom of the piles should be the ones you'll need the least often. Make sure you keep flammable items away from your furnace, hot water heater, washer, dryer, and any other potential heat sources.

Find Each Possession a Home

As you get to work putting your things away in your basement, consider organizing your belongings according to category, such as "holidays," "sports," "memorabilia," and so on. There are some items that might be in your basement for purely sentimental reasons. If you need to hold on to these items, there are a few things you could do to reduce the physical space they consume.

For starters, you can create a memorabilia box for each family member. Whatever the size of the box, seek to limit the amount of items saved to what you could fit in that box. Ideally, the box would be plastic to protect fragile items. While it can be worthwhile to hold on to items of sentimental value, it's best to put some kind of system into place that will force you to be selective. Another idea is to take a picture of items that have sentimental value but you know will never have a place in your home. Instead of holding on to the actual item, you can hold on to the photo (or better yet—you can store the image on your computer). This compromise will allow you to retain a link to the memory or person that the item represents without using precious storage.

Here are some guidelines for storing items:

- Clean, package, and/or launder the items. Items that go into storage in good condition are more apt to stay that way longer. Polish your jewelry or silver flatware before storing it.

- Categorize.

- Sort and place similar items together.

- Place items in appropriate (airtight) storage containers, which come in a variety of sizes.

- Label. Mark each carton, container, or item with a descriptive label that's easily visible. For example, "Summer Clothing," "Baby Clothing," "1998 Personal Financial Records," "Christmas Decorations," or "Winter Jackets."

- Store items in such a way that they can be easily found and retrieved without your having to dig through endless piles of stuff.

In any hardware store, you'll find a wide range of plastic and metal shelving units, some that are standalone units and others that need to be bolted and installed directly onto your walls. After you decide what smaller items you'll be keeping and what you will store in your basement, choose the best method for storing these smaller items, using boxes, shelving, cabinets, or perhaps a pegboard with hooks that gets mounted on a wall.

Seasonal Organization

As you decide where your various items will be stored, think in terms of when they'll be used. For example, you may want to store your winter clothing in containers near your holiday decorations. Likewise, you may want to store your grill near your Fourth of July decorations and lawn furniture. If you tend to go on a family vacation every summer (and use your luggage), you may want to store your luggage near your summer items for easy access.

Your most frequently used items should receive prime storage space so they're most readily accessible any time of the year. If you also use your basement as a workshop, exercise room, or hobby area, make sure your storage area is kept separate. You can use room dividers or other methods to section off each area of your basement as needed.

Down and Out

Remember, what happens downstairs affects what goes on upstairs. When you turn your basement into a storage graveyard, you bury opportunities to breathe out the living quarters in other areas of your home. Make it a point to take periodic inspections of what you've got and what you can get rid of. Then keep areas zoned out, no matter what type of basement you have, to keep the space functioning in a way that supports the smooth running of your household. With the right strategies in place in a finished basement, you will not only be able to accommodate a range of different activities and hobbies, but members of your household will also be able to engage in those activities simultaneously.

part 4

work and play

Oftentimes, your home does double duty. It's not just where you live, it's where you work. It's not just where you watch TV at night or entertain, it's where you raise your children. When you add these extra dimensions to the way your home functions, you also add the potential for additional clutter. Well, not anymore! The following chapters will help you organize your home office and your kids' clutter. It may seem overwhelming, but remember, even if you start slow you'll still make it to the finish line eventually! And without all that clutter holding you back, who knows how far you'll go!

Chapter 14
That's Kid Stuff

AFTER YOU HAVE KIDS, YOUR LIFE IS CHANGED FOREVER. Even before the first little one arrives, gifts from friends and family start to pile up. As the accoutrements accumulate, you can't help but feel overwhelmed, especially if you're striving for a clutter-free home. The key is to create a kid-friendly workspace that's childproof when necessary and organized always. Mission impossible? Not necessarily. For games, toys, stuffed animals, supplies, and management of big, messy craft projects, read on for creative ideas you can deploy quickly and inexpensively. This chapter explores the task of creating and organizing a kid-friendly room, as well as balancing their possessions and your peace of mind.

Toy Stories

A playroom? You may be thinking your whole house is one big playroom. There are toys in the living room, board games in the basement, and stuffed animals on the stairs. Oh, and is that last night's science experiment on the kitchen table?

According to the Toy Industry Association, toys are a $20 billion annual business, making it larger than the video game, domestic motion-picture box office, and music industries. If you're like most parents, there may be days when you feel as though you're single-handedly responsible for keeping those toy companies afloat.

The Bottom Line

Toy industry analysts point to a trend known in the business as KGOY. It stands for "kids getting older younger." It's a theory that says kids are not only becoming increasingly more sophisticated in their use of technology, they're consuming more mature entertainment at younger and younger ages.

Having too many toys is one problem, and having too many pieces is another. A big frustration, says one exhausted mom, is that something is missing from every toy and game in her house. Pull out a Barbie doll, and she's got just one shoe. Play Scrabble, and the Z is missing. Puzzle pieces go AWOL and are never seen again. If your home doesn't have a dedicated playroom, every room becomes a playroom, and the entire house suffers. Suddenly, you feel like your nice adult habitat has been taken over by little squatters—who happen to have *big* sprawling needs. It's time to regain control.

To begin, you need to carve out a space and give the kids a home of their own. If you have a spare room in the house, great. Otherwise, think about the best spot to dedicate to a play area. Of course, that doesn't mean there won't be spillover. Kids are kids, after all. They have a tendency to spread out their toys in different rooms and leave them there. However, giving them their own place bestows a sense of ownership and permanence. It lets them know there's a place where their things belong. One family tried by dedicating a sun porch to their two daughters, but the quantity of toys got so out of hand they took up the entire room. The kids actually needed to find another room in which to play.

Watch Out!

Kids love stuffed animals, but according to the Green Guide, the newsletter covering health and environmental issues, the cottons, synthetics, and wools used in the stuffing may contain insecticide residue and dyes, which can be carcinogenic. Toys using organic, toxic-free materials are available from a growing number of companies, including Organic Gift Shop (*www.organicgiftshop.com*) and Mama's Earth (*www.mamasearth.com*).

Here are a few possibilities for play areas:

- Basement
- Den
- Enclosed porch
- Finished attic
- Great room
- Guest bedroom

Any of these rooms can be zoned off as play areas, even if it's just a chunky, oversize corner. The trick is to make sure the area is clearly delineated. Be inventive. You can use paint, drapes, a piece of furniture, or decorative screen panels to mark the territory, or even be whimsical by using beaded curtains or a hammock filled with stuffed animals to define the space.

Don't underestimate the power of a well-decorated room to create an environment in which your children will want to work, play, and dream. A wall dominated with a blackboard or bulletin board can become an ever-evolving backdrop that reflects your child's changing tastes, hobbies, interests, and creativity. Also, even though your child might be the cause of the mess, you might be surprised by how joyfully many kids react to an orderly environment, especially when you allow them to help develop a system of organization.

Now, before you move all the old toys over to the new play space, give them a good looking-over. If your child has more toys than Santa's workshop, you've got your work cut out for you. The hardest part is going through all the little pieces associated with so many games. No one has to tell you how maddening it can be to match parts without mixing them all up. If you start feeling overwhelmed, take the task in small doses, a couple of hours at a time, suggests organizing expert Heidi Gaumet. But if you tackle it that way, make sure you separate out what's already been organized so you don't wind up duplicating efforts.

Keep these details in mind as you do your sorting:

- Relocate games your child isn't old enough to play with to a long-term storage area such as a basement, attic, or closet. Just don't leave them there forever!

- Separate the toys you want to save for sentimental reasons, and store them elsewhere in a special container or chest.

- Discard all games with missing pieces, stuffed animals that have seen better days, and toys no longer in working order.

- Throw out any books with torn, tattered, or chocolate-smeared pages.

- Donate items your child has outgrown, has multiples of, or has lost interest in.

Put a limit on saving items that have sentimental value. Oddly enough, it's the parents—not the kids—who are often reluctant to get rid of old toys. One mom still saves the storybooks she read to her son when he was a toddler, even though he's preparing for college. That same mom didn't keep such a good eye on a cherished heirloom rocking horse, though. It was accidentally donated to a neighbor, and the disappointed mom wound up having to buy it back a year later for $25 at the neighbor's garage sale.

An Organized Inquiry

What's the best way to preserve toys that have sentimental value? You can create a memory box to hold special items and turn the production of the box into a family project at the same time. Visit your local crafts store and pick up a plain wooden box. Then use your imagination to decorate it with family photos and personal objects so that both the box and its contents can be family heirlooms.

If any items are brand new and still in their original packaging, donate them to a local children's hospital or save them for a holiday toy drive.

If you're on the fence about whether to give away something your youngster might want down the road, you can always pack it up and put it in storage temporarily. Wait about six months, and if your child hasn't asked for it, feel free to give it away.

Get the Kids Involved

Should you or shouldn't you? Let your child become involved in the weeding and sorting process, that is. The answer is a definitive maybe. You might have a clear idea about which playthings your child is using, but she might not be ready to part with any of them. Avoid putting yourself in a situation in which a sorting session can degenerate into tears and tantrums—and not necessarily your child's. Purging and organizing can be stressful enough. What's more, you and your child are likely to have different concerns. You're more focused on issues of safety and neatness. Your little one has one desire: to get at the goods.

On the other hand, if you think your child is mature enough to be part of the decision-making process, it could be a great way to introduce him to a lifelong lesson in personal organization. Incorporate him in the process, and he'll be more motivated to keep it up. It'll also show him you respect his space and belongings. Figuring out the right age isn't an exact science. Try it, but be patient. The tools you employ in the playroom might be a bit overwhelming for a young mind.

Watch Out!

Like father, like son; like mother, like daughter—your kids will follow your cues when it comes to organization. If the rest of the rooms in your home are cluttered and your tabletops are stacked high with messy piles, chances are your children are going to pick up your bad habits and follow suit. If you set an example, you'll have an easier time helping them keep their playrooms neat and tidy.

Misha Keefe, professional organizer, recommends thinking in thirds. When it comes to toys, keep a third, purge a third, and store a third. Then every few months, take out those stored toys and put them in rotation. Your child will feel like she's getting new toys on a regular basis.

As you start moving items into place, break down the area into three separate zones: one for play; another for creative ventures like art, crafts, and science projects; and a third reserved for quiet study, homework, and reading. The zones don't have to be elaborate to be functional. Keep in mind that clutter affects children as well as adults. It's distracting and stressful. The trouble is, kids can't articulate their response to a messy environment, so it's up to you to be aware.

Post-Holiday Purge

A simple way to start getting your kids involved is to use the holidays as a reason for them to clean out their space. Try doing either a pre- or post-holiday purge. Let your child know that presents are coming and that he is going to need space for all those gifts. Your child can help make space by letting go of a few items. You might try leaving a box in your child's room marked "Give away" and let him slowly fill that box. Sometimes it is not just the idea of getting rid of things that can be disturbing to a child, but also the quick pace that his parents use for such efforts. By leaving the box in his room, you allow him to take his time and make thoughtful decisions about what stays and what goes.

If you want to sweeten the bait a bit, let your child know that every item he places in the box is likely to be replaced over the course of the holiday season. Especially if your family is large and into gift-giving, it is safe to assume that no matter how many items your child decides to purge, more will come in than go out.

Word to the Wise

While your child anticipates his holiday gifts, many children around the world have little to look forward to. You may want to encourage your child by explaining how much joy he can bring to others by sifting through his things and picking some high-quality, gently used items to share.

One of the reasons that clutter so easily gets out of control is that we forget to expect it. Certain seasons of life invite clutter. If you're preparing to bring a new baby into the home, for example, you can expect that, although your baby will be small, baby items can easily overwhelm a small space, especially if you haven't taken time to empty out drawers and shelves before the big event.

Ideally, before a holiday, the birth of a child, the start of the school year, or any event or season that is sure to bring more material items into your home, you can prepare by making space. If you can keep a few empty drawers available, more stuff doesn't have to mean more stress. With a little bit of planning, you can create space for your child's room to grow with his needs.

Changing Times

Keep in mind that storage requirements change from year to year as kids grow. A toddler's needs and interests are different from a kindergartener's. Fast-forward a few years, and that same youngster is now a teen whose room might very well be overwhelmed with schoolbooks, trophies, sports gear, and instruments. Keep it simple. Straightforward solutions are the easiest for kids to follow at any age. Take advantage of vertical space, but you might want to consider a youngster's perspective and arrange items in the room at a lower level than you would for adults.

There are a few storage solutions that cut across all ages. Baskets, for instance, are stylish, multifunctional, and available in a wide range of sizes to fit all needs. Never mind the lids. Open baskets make it easier to see what's inside, and lids wind up adding to the clutter. Sturdiness is always the name of the game. Make sure your containers are up for the punishment kids have to give them. Anything tippy or wobbly has to go. See-through bins will help a child spend less time hunting and more time playing and creating. Repurpose plastic shoe boxes for Barbie dolls, action figures, and model kit parts.

If there's one area ripe for innovation, this is it. Not long ago, Tupperware held its first ever Global Design contest. Entrants from the United States, Latin America, Europe, Asia, and the Middle East produced artistic and functional products out of Tupperware. One of the winners, a Tupperware saleswoman from Brazil, took a top-selling bowl and created a clown-shaped toy trunk out of it to hold toys, games, and crayons. The clown trunk was even displayed in a special exhibition at an art gallery in Manhattan.

The Bottom Line

The U.S. Consumer Product Safety Commission is charged with protecting the public from risks of serious injury or death from thousands of types of consumer products. To find out if a toy or children's product has been recalled, visit *www.cpsc.gov*. It's a good idea to keep this site on your list of website favorites.

High-placed shelves are an attractive way to keep fragile items out of harm's way while giving special items like precious collectibles, awards, toy models, and even beloved stuffed animals the spotlight they deserve.

Can't control the stuffed animal population? Plush toy "zoos" are ideal solutions. Flexible bars allow kids to move their favorites in and out, and yet the collection is neatly contained in a fanciful cage.

Throw a decorative swatch of material over a worktable, and you'll have a hidden storage area underneath.

Is there a closet in the room you can co-opt? You might want to forgo the hangers and install adjustable shelving instead. Hang a shoe organizer with multiple clear pockets over the closet door, and you've got lots of pouch-size homes for everything from hair clips to vacation souvenirs.

Word to the Wise

Lots of board games come in oversize packaging that uses up unnecessary storage space. Shrink games down to size by removing the plastic, foam, cardboard inserts, and superfluous boxes. Then store game parts in small see-through stackable bins or zip-close bags.

Plan intuitively by remembering to store items closest to their points of usage. Paper, books, and stationery supplies should be near the work desk; art supplies go by the crafts table; puzzles and board games by the game table. That'll make it easier for kids to put things back where they belong when they're done. Is there a would-be Picasso in the family? Instead of burying her works of art in drawers, hang a clothesline to display them for an instant art gallery and a giant splash of color.

If you have more than one child sharing the playroom, use color-coded containers to help them find their own toys more easily and nip squabbling in the bud. You can also assign a wall per child so that each one has shelves, bins, and cabinets suited especially for him.

Age-Old Issues

What age, stage, and even what size your child is will determine how her playthings should be organized. For the preschool crowd, take the height and weight of objects into consideration when giving kids access to their things. Realize, too, that storage is a moving target. The height of shelves and storage bins this year may need to be adjusted before you know it. Storage is impractical, even counterproductive, when it doesn't fit a youngster's needs. Kids don't play with toys they can't see or reach. If you stack toys too high, they're liable to become dust collectors. Or worse: They'll become temptations. The last thing you want is your child climbing chairs, furniture, or windowsills to get at something enticing.

The Bottom Line

The popularity of some toys never wanes. Classic toys that are still on the market more than a century after they were created include Parcheesi, Lionel Trains, teddy bears, Crayola Crayons, and the Model T Ford, the first die-cast toy car. Parcheesi, by Milton Bradley, was first introduced in 1867.

To guard against a potential choking hazard situation, keep toys and games with small parts off limits unless there's adult supervision. These items should be stowed in closets on high shelves or in cabinets with child locks. Toy chests aren't always a good idea at this age, either. A heavy lid can gobble up tiny fingers.

All storage units should be clearly marked. Use identifiers that young children can easily understand. If they're too young to read labels, employ a color-coding system. Try red bins, for instance, for dolls; blue for puzzles. Better still, create a label for each container with a picture of the item. Overcomplicate your organizational system, and you'll have a system destined to stall.

Last Resorts

The only way to keep clutter at bay is to keep it moving, especially when you realize how quickly it accumulates. If, despite your best efforts, your child is still a bit of a hoarder and you cannot compel her to place items in the give-away box, you may need to try one of two approaches.

One approach, advocated by the book *Parenting with Love and Logic* by Foster Kline and Jim Fay, is to teach your child to become responsible for her own items. This approach requires a bit of "tough love." Instead of yelling and complaining about messes in your child's room, you can tell her that if she doesn't keep toys and clothes off the floor, those items might just disappear one day.

Especially when your child is small, you'll want to help her work out organizational systems that are logical for her. It is reasonable for her to ask for and expect your help. But as she matures, challenge her to take ownership of her own room.

This approach has two great benefits: it teaches the child to be responsible for her own items a lesson that lasts a lifetime—and it allows the parents to delegate. A parent who can share the work of home organizing with his child is less likely to feel overwhelmed. A child who feels that she has a share in the household is also likely to feel a boost in her self-image. If you take opportunities to help your child cultivate these kinds of skills, she will be better able to manage her home as an adult.

Another—more sneaky—approach is to use those hours when your child is away at school to declutter the room yourself. This is especially recommended for younger children, who are less likely to be upset by a feeling of having their personal boundaries crossed. When children are older, you'll want to work with them to help them purge. As they age, any "invasion" into their rooms when they're not there will be taken as a betrayal.

The Bottom Line

Although it could be devastating for your child to find that some of her toys have disappeared, it will be more draining for you, over the long haul, to always have to pick up after her. If you follow through with the threat, you'll be surprised at how much more consistent your child will become in her cleaning habits.

Especially when children are small, you may be able to cart off toys, clothing, and the like without them noticing. You may fear that they'll come home and be devastated by the results of your purge, but instead find that they (like you) are just happy to be in a place that is less cluttered.

Often, after you carry off a few bags of their items, children discover toys that they had forgotten. Many young children will spend hours quietly "rediscovering" their more precious toys that may have been obscured by the clutter. It can be a great joy, for both parents and children, to finally be able to appreciate what they have instead of always thinking in terms of more. Clutter invites more clutter. Things don't look (or feel) right, so you're tempted to try to buy additional things to fix the problem. In an orderly and serene environment, however, contentment will come naturally.

If you're living in a tight space, consider the following space-saving options:

- Add hooks on the closet door(s) and inside the closet (on the side walls) for jackets, shoe bags, and other items.

- Free up valuable floor space by utilizing a loft bed for your child. The sleeping area is on the top, while a desk, dresser, shelves, or other forms of storage space can be built beneath the bed.

- If you need to accommodate more than one child in a room, get bunk beds.

- Install shelving on the walls, as opposed to using a freestanding shelf unit that takes up floor space. On these shelves, store books, toys, collectibles, trophies, and other items.

- Install underbed drawers and use underbed storage bins for off-season clothing, toys, sports equipment, and so on. It may make sense to raise the bed slightly to create additional underbed storage.

- Keep furniture to a minimum. Whenever possible, choose pieces of furniture designed for multiple uses. For example, some children's beds already have shelving or drawers built in.

- Make full use of closet organization tools to best utilize closet space.

- Take advantage of the storage space that a good-sized toy chest provides. This can be a central location where toys are kept. Within the toy chest, use plastic bins or shoe boxes to separate toys with lots of small pieces, such as building blocks, toy cars, board games, action figures, dolls (and accessories), and trading cards.

- Display shelving can sometimes be installed about a foot down from the ceiling line. You can use this shelf space to show off collections, trophies, artwork, and other items that don't need to be readily accessed.

Although basic organization can go a long way toward helping your child live more fully in her space, you can also choose items carefully to best serve the space your child inhabits. Finding the furniture that's well built, functional, visually appealing, durable, and within your budget requires searching. Be prepared to visit a number of furniture stores to see the available options. If this furniture will be used by young children, pay careful attention to the quality of construction and think in terms of product safety.

If you're budget-conscious, shop around by visiting your local furniture retailers (including children's-furniture specialty stores and department stores), and then use the Internet to compare prices from online retailers. It's not a good idea, however, to purchase children's furniture you haven't seen, touched, and examined firsthand.

Watch Out!

Don't try to save money by purchasing poor-quality furniture or secondhand furniture (especially for an infant or toddler) that may not meet the latest safety guidelines issued by the U.S. Consumer Product Safety Commission (*www.cpsc.gov/cpscpub/pubs/chld_sfy.html*).

No matter where you buy furniture, keep the following tips in mind:

- Figure out your budget and time frame.
- Decide on a basic look, style, or theme.
- As you see what's available, compare value, workmanship, durability, and safety features.
- Keep storage capabilities foremost in mind.

You can utilize several different types of storage in a bedroom, including open storage (shelves and baskets), closed storage (armoires, bins, chests, underbed storage, and dressers), convenient storage (closets), and remote storage (closets and storage options in other areas of your home, such as the basement, attic, or garage).

Make sure the individual pieces of furniture you choose will fit properly into the layout (both size and décor) of the room as well as into your budget. For example, if you're purchasing a large dresser, is there ample room to open the dresser drawers? After you know the exact measurements of the bedroom as well as the individual pieces of furniture you're interested in, sketch out on paper the room's proposed layout.

Fun and Games

The core issue when it comes to playroom clutter, like other rooms in the house, is overconsumption. Get a handle on that, and you're on your way to streamlined bliss. A surefire way to maintain the momentum is to recycle toys on a regular basis. Your child outgrows toys as quickly as he outgrows clothes. Teach him to let go. Donate items or discard them, but don't let them loiter. Otherwise, the stockpiles will just continue to grow.

Stick with the basic principles of matching the storage unit to the task as well as your child's abilities. Keep up with an easy-to-master labeling system, use easy-access storage containers, make sure things are put away on a daily basis, and you'll have a proper playroom—and your tidy home back, too. The other big benefit to getting your clutter under control is the lesson you teach your kids and the good habits you instill. As with all organizational skills, if you teach children at a young age, they'll reap the benefits into adulthood.

Chapter 15

Office Organization

WHILE SOME PEOPLE BASE THEIR FULL-TIME CAREERS IN THEIR HOMES, others simply need a space to keep records, bills, and related paperwork in order. After all, it's easy to get swallowed up in mounds of bills, letters, cards, and sticky notes (not to mention the electronic clutter of computer components). But whatever your needs are, you can expect that these areas of your home will attract clutter and chaos. This chapter will offer advice on how to create and maintain an orderly home office. A comfortable, functional home office can increase your productivity and your impetus to get things done. This chapter will explore a variety of home-office spaces, as well as offering practical tips for keeping your office in order.

What Are Your Needs?

Before you begin to design and organize your home-office environment, create a detailed list of the types of work you'll be doing there. Keep in mind that you'll want to create a space where you'll want to be. For example, will the work require silence or should your office be located near the front door because of work-related visitors?

Those who work from home (and even those who simply pay bills and sort records there) know that it can be hard enough to motivate yourself to meet your goals. Don't add an extra reason to dread your job by placing your office in a dingy basement. Or if your job requires silence, don't place your desk in a household hub.

After you determine what tasks you hope to accomplish on an ongoing basis in the home office, develop a detailed list of furniture, equipment, and supplies required to achieve your objective. As you determine what's needed, think about ways you can reduce clutter in your workspace. For example, select furniture with plenty of drawers and filing cabinets with extra storage space. You should also position equipment close to electrical outlets and phone jacks, so you won't have lots of unsightly and disorganized cords running throughout the room.

Because your desk is the central and most integral part of your home office, decide on its location first. Then determine what other furniture and equipment needs to be nearby and what can be placed elsewhere in the room. This will help you create the most functional design and layout for your work environment.

Word to the Wise

Julie Morgenstern suggests that if you generate your income through a variety of different types of home-based work, think in terms of creating activity hubs within your office. That way, you'll be better able to assign "homes" to the items associated with your different jobs, and you'll also increase your productivity by "visiting" each area daily.

Once you have a basic idea of what you hope to accomplish in your home workspace and what equipment you'll need in order to achieve your objectives, design and lay out your home office so that it will maximize your productivity and be a comfortable place to work. Issues such as lighting, color schemes, ergonomics, and functionality all need to be addressed. As with any organizational task, planning is crucial, so put some thought into your needs and wants, and then address each issue individually.

Before making a major financial investment in remodeling an area of your home to transform it into a home office, try working in the area for a while to ensure that the environment and surroundings will help you maximize your productivity. Certain problems, such as noise, traffic, or lack of natural light, could remain even if you remodel, so take care to select an area that you like being in.

Remember, you need to pinpoint an area of your home that will provide ample space and the best possible environment (in terms of lighting, temperature, privacy, and sound) for you to be productive. After you know what furniture you'll need, take measurements to make sure that the furniture you're planning to use will fit properly in your current or proposed home office.

Choosing a Desk and Storage Supplies

The most important piece of furniture in any home office is the desk. You want your desk to be functional and comfortable, just the right height so that you don't have to hunch over it, and with enough space to spread out your papers.

As you choose a desk, consider U-shaped or L-shaped designs that provide ample space for a computer, lamp, papers, telephone, etc., but also give you space to do your work. If you incorporate a computer desk into your home office, make sure it's ergonomically designed. The ideal height of the keyboard should be about twenty-eight inches, yet the monitor should be at eye level so that you're not looking up or down at it.

The desk design you ultimately choose should be based upon what you'll be using the desk for. For example, if you'll be holding business meetings around your desk, you'll need ample room for chairs on both sides of the desk, plus a clear line of sight to the people sitting opposite you.

The Bottom Line

If you have bulky supplies in your office that you use rarely, perhaps you should move them into accessible storage. For printers, scanners, and other electronic equipment, purchase a cabinet where you can tuck these items away—just be sure that your storage cabinet has decent ventilation, as electrical items do need air to circulate around them.

For most people, desk space is a priority. Thus, you want to have at your disposal as much open desk space as possible, based on the amount of room in your home office. Take measurements and create your own blueprint on paper. This will allow you to experiment with different room designs so you can have the largest desk possible, yet not feel as if this piece of furniture dominates the room or makes for a claustrophobic workspace. Most home organizers recommend that you position your desk first and then arrange other pieces of furniture around it.

Creative Storage

Be sure to utilize the available space to its greatest potential. For example, instead of having file bins on your desk, can you utilize hanging files and take advantage of nearby wall space? A computer-monitor stand with a shelf above and a drawer underneath it is also an excellent tool for saving valuable desk space. This type of stand will ensure that your computer monitor will be at eye level, and thus inflict less stress on your neck, shoulders, and arms.

Office supplies, shipping supplies, and other items should be readily available. Consider purchasing drawer organizers to keep your office tools compartmentalized. For bulky items like industry magazines and articles, consider dual-function furniture—perhaps you can store these inside an ottoman with a pull-off top.

Broken Records

To determine what you actually need in your office, get rid of the dead weight that's been fattening up drawers, files, and shelves. Even people who pride themselves on their proficiency in filing every record in its rightful folder rarely revisit those files down the road. As a result, filing cabinets and drawers turn into one-way streets of document excess and distress.

An Organized Inquiry

How can I decrease the volume of junk mail being delivered to my home? Junk mail is an ongoing source of irritation for most consumers and a major contributor to paper pileups in the home. Have your name removed from certain mailing lists by signing up online, at *www.dmachoice.org*, or by writing to Direct Marketing Association Mail Preference Service, P.O. Box 643, Carmel, NY 15012.

There's no getting around it. Clearing the clutter starts with a big-time purge session. In the office, don't just focus on the piles on the floor and around your desk. Empty out your drawers, vacate your cabinets, and gut your folders. Depending on the state of the office and how long it's been since you last gave it a thorough going-over, plan to allot anywhere from four to twenty hours for the cleanup. Need some encouragement? Pick a clutter buddy who will keep you focused.

Divide and Conquer

For the purge session, arm yourself with file folders, markers, a few cartons for sorting, and a cache of big trash bags. Mark the first carton ACTION. Go through your paperwork, and put each slip of paper in your ACTION carton if it represents any of the following:

- A pending project

- An ongoing project

- A specific issue that requires your attention

Filling out the rebate form for the scanner you just bought or completing the application for the bank certificate of deposit you've wanted to open for a while are good candidates for your action file.

Mark another carton for FILING. These are the documents you need to save but don't necessarily need to act on. Among other things, they include these:

- Credit card statements

- Bank statements

- Canceled checks

- Tax receipts

- Health care records

- Insurance forms

Here's where we run into the number-one clutter problem. Everyone's got files, but most people don't have a proper filing system. The one they have is outdated, underutilized, and therefore ineffective. Creating a manageable filing system is the single best thing you can do to control papers. It doesn't have to be complicated. In fact, the simpler it is, the better. Organizing authority Ariane Benefit says a lot of her clients "complexify." They create Byzantine systems with too many subcategories and then have a hard time remembering where anything is.

If you start overcomplicating your system, rather than going with a plan that's intuitive and easy to follow, you'll wind up tripping yourself up. One method is to set up files by main categories, such as Home, Automotive, Finance, Health, Insurance, and so on. You can create one file for each topic and then subdivide as needed. One automotive file might be enough for, say, maintenance records, but owning several cars might warrant a separate file for each vehicle. Try not to create too many, though. It's easier to go through twenty files than 200 when you're searching for something. For easier identification, it's helpful to code your files by using colored folders or labels. All health-related folders could be blue, for example, with bank statements red, investment documents yellow, and so on.

Another method is using a straightforward A–Z filing system. There's no one-size-fits-all way. Neither are there one-size-fits-all folders. Match the folder to fill the need. Some papers are better off in see-through folders, others, like thicker documents, in expandable portfolios. Pendaflex, a major manufacturer of office products, offers solutions and lots of sympathy at its free I Hate Filing Club, online at *www.pendaflex.com*.

Word to the Wise

Before you put anything in the to-be-filed carton, make sure you've got a reason to keep it. Conquer your fear of letting go. There's virtually no chance you'll ever need those Christmas gift receipts from three years ago. There's even less chance that you'll need that cable TV bill from 1994.

And then there's the matter of unnecessary layers of backup. You're saving your electric utility statement, plus you've still got your canceled checks? Ask yourself why, especially considering how unlikely it is that you'll ever need proof of payment in the first place. Instead of saving it now only to deal with it later, get into the mindset of assuming that incoming papers are disposable, unless there's a good reason to think otherwise.

Letter Perfect

Keep important documents in a secure lockbox, such as a fireproof home safe. These are the hard-to-replace items you don't necessarily need to access on a regular basis. Among them are the following:

- Wills

- Title to your vehicles

- Stock and bond certificates

- Home and life insurance policies

- Contracts

- Passports

- Marriage license

- Social security cards

- Birth certificates

Having them all together in one grab-and-go box is a sensible precaution should you ever need to leave your home in an emergency. Alternatively, you might want to consider renting a safety deposit box at your local bank.

Papers with sentimental value—those important documents, cards, and letters you want to preserve for the long haul—should be stored in archival-quality boxes or wrapped in acid-free tissue instead of in standard folders. Paper is brittle and has a finite lifespan. It breaks down over time. Heat and humidity hasten the deterioration. Even everyday handling can harm it.

Reserve a box or special envelope exclusively to hold all invitations you receive and/or tickets for airline flights, sporting events, concerts, or shows. When the date arrives, you won't waste time checking every drawer in the house wondering where you left them.

Filing Cabinets

Filing cabinets come in a wide range of sizes. Use as much vertical space as possible by investing in a four-drawer vertical file cabinet. This takes up the least amount of actual floor space, yet can store the most papers. Your most time-sensitive and important papers can be kept directly on your desk using a desktop file holder. It's common for people to utilize an in box or to-do file directly on their desks. The trick, however, is to be disciplined enough to process those important papers promptly, so that they don't accumulate and become unmanageable.

Watch Out!

Avoid cheap filing cabinets. Filing cabinets need to be durable enough to endure years of use and the weight of your paperwork. Cheap filing cabinets come apart over time or become difficult to open and close. Reduce the temptation to put off filing by purchasing filing cabinets that are a joy to use.

Use separate file cabinets for your personal and business files. Next, divide up your files and label them carefully. For example, in your personal filing cabinet, you may have folders or separate files for the following types of paperwork: auto-related, banking, bills, career, education, financial, health/medical, insurance, investments, legal, mortgage, taxes (keeping current and past information separate), travel, and warranties/receipts/instructions.

All of your files should be divided up, labeled, and kept organized. Files can be sorted and stored alphabetically, numerically, with some sort of color-coding, by date, geographically, by subject, or by using your own criteria. Keep your filing system straightforward, up-to-date, and intuitive for others. For example, if you're storing company files, store them alphabetically by company name (or the client's last name).

Keep current files readily available, and keep dormant/inactive files in airtight storage containers in an out-of-the way area, such as a basement or attic. Old files can also be scanned into a computer and stored on a computer's hard drive or in an electronic format, which will save you space and eliminate clutter. An inexpensive document scanner can dramatically simplify this task.

Word to the Wise

Set aside fifteen minutes a week to purge old files that you no longer need. In most cases, you don't need to save earlier drafts of proposals or projects. Check with your accountant to determine how frequently bills, canceled checks, and tax records can be purged.

Dozens, perhaps hundreds of papers will cross your desk each day. For those papers that deserve your utmost attention, that can't be forgotten, or that you classify as having top priority, consider placing a special file on your desk or hanging a bulletin board near your desk upon which you can stick only the most important of papers. You can also digitize them!

Digitize to Downsize

The best way to cut down on paperwork is to digitize it. Scan it and discard the original, whenever possible. A 100 percent paperless work environment might not be a realistic goal—at least not yet—but thinking in bits and bytes means less maintenance and easier document access. Of course, you'll need a system to back up your files, music, and pictures. A number of options are available, from external ZIP disc drives and data sticks or cards, to CDs and DVDs, to web-based file storage programs.

At the speedy pace of technological advancements, you'll need to keep tabs on the latest platforms. If you used to back up onto floppy discs, for instance, you remember having to make the change to CDs or DVDs when you found that your next computer would not have a floppy disc drive. The solution, however, is not to keep your old equipment around to access isolated files. The answer is to transfer them from old platforms to newer, more efficient ones.

When saving files on a CD or DVD, make sure the discs are clearly labeled and placed in a plastic jewel case. Discs are best stored in a cool, dark place. Stick with high-quality brand-name CDs. If a CD becomes scratched, it can become unusable. One more thing: Avoid backing up crucial information on a rewritable CD. If you do, you might unwittingly use that same CD for another application and accidentally rewrite over your data.

Writer Moira Allen first created an archival system to back up her tax records. It's a smart idea as protection from a home emergency or disaster, but Moira had another motivation in mind. She moved nine times over the course of twenty years and was looking for any means to lighten her load. After the tax returns, she backed up all her important personal documents. Keep in mind that scanned copies of business receipts and tax records are acceptable by the Internal Revenue Service. On the other hand, scanned birth certificates, passports, deeds, marriage licenses, and the like are not considered valid documents. It still makes sense to digitize them. A scanned copy will contain all the information you need should you ever have to replace the originals.

Word to the Wise

When you're ready to upgrade your computer, avoid having your old unit wind up in a landfill. It's becoming one of the nation's fastest-growing environmental concerns. Many computer manufacturers will accept computers for recycling for a nominal fee or, sometimes, free of charge. Schools, charities, and even some prisons will accept donations of no-longer-used computers and electronics.

While you're at it, declutter your computer's hard drive, too, by defragging. Over time, files get scattered around your hard drive, causing your computer to work twice as hard to access them. By running the disc defragmenter software utility, you're simply organizing all your files in way that makes it easier for the computer to locate them. If you're the type of person who installs and uninstalls programs frequently, you should defrag every couple of weeks. Otherwise, once a month is good enough. You should see a noticeable boost in speed.

Want to cut down on all the little notes and long lists you leave for yourself to remind you about birthdays, meetings, and events? Try some of the free online date-book tools, like AOL's Remind Me, Yahoo! Calendar, and HappyBirthday.com, and you'll never have to apologize for your bad memory again.

Keep at It

Keep in mind that organization is an ongoing process. Once you have your system up and running, keep up with it. Ongoing maintenance, just a few minutes a day, is the answer to avoiding a relapse of the paper chokehold. Put things where they belong as soon as you're done with them. Exorcising files from folders from time to time is the perfect exercise for multitaskers. When you're watching TV or waiting for the water in the teapot to boil, grab some folders and pore through them, weeding out old documents or moving them to long-term storage elsewhere in your home. The time you devote to office organization today, even ten minutes a day, is an investment toward the hours you'll spend tomorrow.

After all, after you've had an opportunity to tackle the clutter and to bring the tools you need into your office, you might find that you actually have to work less, and yet your productivity naturally increases. When you don't have to chase down paperwork or dig for contact information, small tasks can be done swiftly and you'll have more energy and time to devote to the more essential and lucrative tasks.

part 5

take it outside

All over America, garages and storage sheds are bursting at the seams with clutter. Many cars are relegated to driveways because of all the things stashed in the garage. Shovels and rakes litter your yard or lean up against your shed because there's no space for them inside. Cluttered garages and sheds are costly—cars and tools forced to sleep outside won't have the lifespan of their garage- or shed-protected counterparts. They quickly rust and are more likely to be stolen by inquisitive passersby. In this part, you'll learn how to maximize your outdoor spaces and make room to bring your belongings in from the cold.

TAKE IT OUTSIDE

Chapter 16
Enjoy a Glorious Garage

WANT TO ACTUALLY HAVE ROOM IN YOUR GARAGE FOR A CAR? For many homeowners, that's a novel notion. Heavy equipment, sporting gear, and even backup appliances have muscled their way in, leaving vehicles often literally out in the cold. In the garage, every surface is a storage opportunity. Wall arrangements don't have to be works of art. They just have to make the space tidy and efficient. Learn about nifty garage solutions that will allow you to have your coupe and park it, too.

Car Wars

Once upon a time, garages were expressly designed to house one thing: the family vehicle. But over the years, they've evolved dramatically into inexpensive yet functional workrooms and recreational spaces. Actually, in some circles they're being called "flexispaces," ready to serve any need for any family member. Some common uses of a garage include the following:

- Tool shed
- Garden center
- Workshop
- Exercise studio
- Garbage and recycling center
- Hobby and crafts workspace
- Children's play room
- Sports equipment area

One South Carolina housewife, thinking about her detached garage with a second story loft, says it houses not only her husband's woodworking shop but a little mirror and basin, too. That's where he trims his beard and moustache so the whiskers don't get all over the bathroom floor!

Wonderful things have been known to happen in garages. Is there something particularly inspiring about them? Something that makes them incubators for great ideas? You'd have to think so, based on some of the fun, funky, and far-reaching concepts that were hatched in garages. Walt Disney is said to have come up with his idea for Mickey Mouse while working in a garage and watching mice at play. The theme song to the old TV show *Gilligan's Island* was recorded in a garage. A couple of Stanford University engineers, Bill Hewlett and David Packard, started Hewlett-Packard in a California garage. And that's exactly where Steve Jobs and Steve Wozniak built their prototype for the first personal computer, the Apple.

There are more than 65 million garages in the United States, according to statistics compiled by GarageTek, a New York–based garage system company. How times have changed! In 1950 nearly 60 percent of new homes were constructed without a garage. Today, garages are virtually a given, with the vast majority housing two cars or more. And like many symbols of status, the bigger the better. In fact, some super-size structures with enough stalls to accommodate multiple vehicles *plus* a golf cart *and* a boat are being dubbed "garage Mahals." The number of garages with three or more bays continues to rise at double-digit rates. The numbers are even more dramatic in those areas of the country where basements are rare and storage space is at a bigger premium.

The Bottom Line

Another popular use for the garage? Band practice. The garage rock movement began in the mid-1960s, when teenagers began appropriating their parents' garages and turning them into rehearsal studios. The term "garage rock" stuck. Bands such as Buddy Holly and the Crickets, The Kinks, Creedence Clearwater Revival, and Nirvana all got their start in the garage.

Central Park

There really is no mystery as to why a garage gets so cluttered up. The answer is quite simple: because it's there. Even for homes with basements or attics, a garage is a lot easier to access. It just calls out to be filled up! And the fuller it becomes, the less likely you'll ever want to deal with the disorganized mess. That 60 percent of homeowners admit to having a very disorganized garage shouldn't come as much of a surprise.

That's why driveways across the country are lined up with cars that no longer fit in the garage. It's no joke. According to one study, a whopping 40 percent of people who own a garage park their car in the driveway. It doesn't make much sense when you think about it. Vehicles valued at $20,000, $30,000, $40,000, or more are left out to brave the elements while beat-up lawn mowers, rarely used bicycles, and spare refrigerators get prime space.

Barry Izsak, president of the National Association of Professional Organizers and author of *Organize Your Garage in No Time*, says the American two-car has become the no-car garage. Don't know what to do with something? Put it in the garage. It's become the family dumping ground, so it's only logical that garages are the places where clutter reaches epic proportions.

There's the story of a cosmetics saleswoman who packed her inventory away in her garage and kept it there for years, even after the dates on her merchandise had long expired. Meanwhile, her husband was a livery driver who bought a new Lincoln Town car every year. The car—representing a big chunk of the couple's livelihood—sat out on the street while the garage protected a load full of useless products.

Word to the Wise

If you need extra shelter for your car, truck, recreation vehicle, or boat, a portable garage might do the trick. Choose from an all-weather model made of plastic sheeting or a metal frame covered in a form-fitting tarp.

Is your garage filled to the brim? Another woman kept an old freezer in her garage packed with meats that had been there so long, they didn't just suffer freezer burn—they were positively polar.

For some reason, we seem to have no compunction about showing our dysfunctional garages to the world. We might shut the door to a messy office or close off any views to a muddled basement, but when it comes to the garage, we open it daily for all the neighborhood to see. Then again, more likely than not, the neighbor's garage is in the same sorry, chaotic state.

The garage is one of the most difficult rooms to organize, and there's a good reason for that. When you move in, it's empty. There's no structure to follow, no blueprint to heed. Think about it. A closet at least has rods and shelves. A kitchen has drawers and cabinets. But in a garage,

ENJOY A GLORIOUS GARAGE

there's *nada*, zilch. You have to create that structure on your own, and the fact is that few people do—or at least do it right.

Garages typically serve multiple functions for different members of the household. Sporting gear and gardening equipment are probably in every garage. That's okay. The good news is that there's room for it and more, if you plan it right. In one survey, more than half the consumers polled said they had plans to reorganize their garage. Well, as the old saying goes, there's no time like the present.

Watch Out!

Ninety-four percent of homeowners store dangerous items in their garages. Always store chemicals in the containers they came in. Keep insecticides, weed killer, and other poisonous chemicals away from the reach of children. Move them to a high shelf or, preferably, into a locked but ventilated cabinet. For questions about the use or disposal of pesticides, contact the National Pesticide Telecommunications Network, at 1-800-858-7378.

But to get from here to there, from clutter and chaos to order and organization, you'll have to roll up your sleeves, don the work clothes, and determine exactly what you've got. Yes, that means it's inventory time again. The key is not to defeat yourself before you get started. You might have five, ten, maybe twenty years or more of accumulated clutter behind those great big garage doors. So set realistic expectations. Pick a nice day, and get down to business.

Get In Gear

Enlist a friend or family member to lend a hand with heavy-lifting duties and, equally important, an objective pair of eyes to help you make the tough decisions about what to keep and what to throw away. If you're one of those people who finds it hard to part with your possessions, you'll find something nice about this process: By taking everything out of the garage for sorting purposes, your things are that much closer to the trash cans.

Use your driveway or an adjacent patio as a staging area, and divide it into zones for items you'll keep, discard, donate, and relocate. If you really have a jam-packed garage, consider PODS, or Portable On-Demand Storage (*www.pods.com*). A weatherproof and secure storage container is delivered to your home, enabling you to temporarily house belongings while you sort through the organizational process.

The Bottom Line

Sears, Roebuck & Co. introduced prefabricated garages and sold mail-order garage kits in the early twentieth century. Those early garages had windows for light and ventilation with doors that swung out like barn doors, instead of up. Some even had doors at both ends so that vehicles could enter from one direction and exit out the other side. No backing out necessary.

Start by getting rid of the obvious stuff that you can easily reach first. That'll help you clear out some space quickly. Then go through the remaining items one at a time. Follow this process:

- Donate anything your family has outgrown—either physically or interest-wise. The garage just isn't the place to hold onto sentimental favorites.

- Find a deserving home for tools that are still in working order but that you've replaced with the latest, greatest version.

- Say *adios* to anything that's been bested by time and humidity.

- Just say no to anything that doesn't belong in a garage.

One dutiful homeowner tried to get rid of the clutter. She'd regularly haul items to the curb for trash pickup, but then her husband would rummage through the piles after dark. The next morning, she inevitably found them right back in the garage.

On the day they moved out of their home, one family made two curious garage discoveries. The first was a pile of newspapers dated July 20, 1969, documenting the first moon landing. Unsurprisingly, after decades kept outside in unsuitable storage conditions, the historical papers were so brittle they disintegrated on touch and had to be tossed. The other surprise was finding a life-size cutout of actress Tuesday Weld that had—for reasons unknown—been won at a church event years earlier. To paraphrase Forrest Gump, a garage is like a box of chocolates. You never know what you're going to get.

Don't Stall Out

By being realistic about what you really need to keep, you've hopefully created an impressive pile for the next trash collection. But before you haul the keepers back into the garage, it's time to put an organizational plan in place.

Word to the Wise

What if the biggest piece of junk in your garage is actually your car? Some clunkers cost more to tow than they're worth on the open market. If that's the case, think about donating your vehicle to a charity. If your wheels are valued at more than $500, the Internal Revenue Service limits your deduction to the charity's actual selling price.

The extent of your storage plan is predicated on how much stuff you have. Want another incentive to downsize? The less stuff you have, the less money you'll need to cough up for storage accessories. Make no mistake about it. The garage is one of the top areas in the home for storage and organizational product spending. It's typically the one place used by the entire family on a regular basis. As a result, consumers have begun making garage organization a priority to the tune of some $800 million in sales, representing about 11 percent of the total organization market. What's more, sales are predicted to grow by 12 to 15 percent.

Don't think of your garage as a mere room, but as a multidimensional storage facility. You've got five sides to work with: the floor, two side walls, a back wall, and a ceiling. Consider location and accessibility when determining the best spots for your items.

The Bottom Line

If your garage feels chaotic, know that you are not alone. Nearly 50 percent of American homeowners who were surveyed admitted that their garage was disorganized, according to the National Association of Professional Home Organizers. One-third of this group added that their garage was the messiest place in their home.

Of course, let's start with a given. The sweet spots of a one, two, or even three-car garage are going to be reserved for—drum roll, please—your vehicles. Then subdivide the remaining space into dedicated zones for each major storage category or activity. Gardening, auto maintenance, home repair, sports, and outdoor entertaining are a few common examples.

While you're starting to organize, keep in mind that your garage is a non–climate-controlled space. You'll want to be very careful about storing items there. Certain items, such as bikes, garden tools, and lawnmowers, are hearty enough to hold up in the garage. Other items—including anything made of cloth or paper—should not be stored in the garage because of the possibility of mold and damage. Ideally, you want to store less in your garage so that the few things you do store there will be readily accessible. Place the items you use the most in the easiest areas to access, making sure they don't interfere with the opening and closing of car or garage doors.

A Good Cleaning

Before you start moving your belongings back into your garage, and before you put your storage solutions in place, take this opportunity to sweep out your garage and give it a good cleaning. Pull down cobwebs, wash windows, and possibly even hose down the floor. Do whatever it takes to make you feel good about your garage. If you'll be parking your car there after you've organized your storage, remember that you may start using it several times a day. You don't want to be inhaling dust, bugs, and mold every time you exit and enter your car.

Word to the Wise

If you must fit two cars into a small garage, try this: Hang two tennis balls from fishing wire, each located to brush the center of your windshield as you pull in. This will help you get each car into the proper spot and prevent you from hitting anything that is stored along the back wall of your garage.

If there are grease spots, you'll want to try to get them up immediately. Concrete floors are porous and the stains can become permanent if you don't tackle them quickly. Although people often neglect the garage floor, spots under your car can provide useful information for troubleshooting problems with your car. If you're leaking oil, you'll want to have your car checked, for example. If you're leaking antifreeze, you'll want to get that leak fixed so that your car doesn't overheat! Consider those spots on the garage floor important tools in diagnosing problems with your car, and try to keep a clean slate so that you can stay on top of potential hazards.

The eHow website (*www.ehow.com*) offers these tips for removing oil stains from your garage or driveway. You may be able to get the oil up with just one or a few of the steps, but if the stain is really bad, you may have to try all of the remedies.

1. Pour cola over the oily areas and let it seep overnight. The following morning, lather some dishwashing liquid in a bucket. Rinse the cola with the soapy water and then hose it off.

2. Next, add baking soda, cornmeal or sawdust to the oily spots. If you're working with a dry stain, wet it so that you'll have a pasty texture when the absorbent powder is added. Then scrub with a brush or broom.

3. Add automatic dishwasher detergent to the spot. You do not need to rise off the baking soda or sawdust. Leave this mixture on the floor for several minutes and then pour boiling water over the area. Scrub with a stiff brush and rinse.

4. If none of these simpler remedies work, purchase a commercial concrete cleaner or grease solvent. Carefully follow the instructions on the container.

5. Follow each remedy by hosing down the area and letting the area air dry.

To prevent oil spots in the future, you can seal your garage floor. This will make it much easier to keep clean and will prevent future stains. If you choose to paint the floor, the sealant can function as a primer. If you do paint, why not use a bold color that you love? You can afford to take color risks in the garage. Also, by adding a color you enjoy to the garage, you may find that it is easier to keep it clean. Dark, dingy spaces provide little inspiration for the ongoing work of organizing and maintaining a space.

EHow offers the following tips for sealing your garage floor:

1. Scrub the floor with a concrete cleaner and degreaser. If the floor has stains, leave the cleaner on for up to 30 minutes before scrubbing. Rinse well.

2. When the floor is dry, put the sealer in a paint tray. Use a paint roller to roll the sealer onto the floor. Slowly work your way out of the garage. Though you want to use a generous amount of sealant, make sure that you remove all puddles. Keep in mind that sealant can also leave stains and that you want to keep your garage door open and run a fan for ventilation.

3. Do not apply a second coat of sealant, but do wash your tools quickly in a bucket of warm, soapy water.

As you clean out your garage, you'll also want to make sure that your drains are functioning well. You'll want to clean them out by hand in the fall and spring, and you may need to bring in a plumber to unclog them if a problem becomes serious. If your garage is attached to your home, a clog could cause flooding, so you'll want to attend to these drains even when they are just becoming slow, but still function. A slow drain can quickly become a completely clogged drain.

Watch Out!

Make sure that all of your garage drains are clear and functioning well. Hosing off the floor will also give you the opportunity to check on the drain efficiency. If they're draining slowly or not at all, you'll want to declog them before you put anything back into your garage.

As you clean your garage and survey the items that have been stored there, take note of any signs of damage done by weather or pests. If there have been pests in your garage, you'll want to greatly reduce the number of items stored in your garage until you're able to identify the problem and solve it. Take note of which items attract pests and which ones suffer damage from the elements, and find a new home for these types of things.

Storage Solutions

After you've organized your belongings into categories, you'll want to begin to plan storage for the items you'll keep there. Keep your garage empty, and drive your car into it. Then take a piece of chalk and outline your car on the floor. Make sure you open the doors of your car to ensure that you leave ample clearance to get in and out of your vehicle(s). Finally, measure the remaining space to determine which types of storage might work for you.

Simple shelving, unobtrusive bins, and shallow closed cabinets can handle a moderate load, provided there are no hoarder types residing at your address. To maintain order, make sure each bin is clearly labeled and filled only with similar items. Dedicate separate containers for garden supplies, tools, sporting equipment, and maintenance products like tool sharpeners, oil, replacement parts, and so on.

Pegboards are tried-and-true resources for housing tools—and then some. Have a board cut to size and then use it to hang wire baskets. It'll help you get protective sports equipment, pool accessories, and toys off the floor. Pegboards with wider holes and larger hooks can hold heavier gear. A simple solution for bulky items like soccer balls and baseball mitts is to place them in mesh bags and then hang them on a pegboard hook. Give new life to household discards by deploying old chests, cabinets, and even entertainment units that have seen better days in the garage for dust-free storage.

If your garage reflects a busy household with family members who have lots of hobbies and all the equipment that goes along with them, it might be time to consider a garage system. Garage systems offer limitless storage possibilities. Some are budget-friendly; others demand more of a deep-pocket investment into the thousands of dollars, depending on the extent of the makeover.

Watch Out!

If you spend a lot of time in your garage doing projects, or if you store fragile items in there, an insulated garage door will provide better protection from extreme temperatures for both you and your possessions. You'll get the added advantage of soundproofing, too—something your neighbors will appreciate if you're on close terms with your high-decibel power tools.

There are high-performance shelving systems with hooks, shelf baskets, and brackets that can be mixed and matched to suit your needs. GarageTek, the Long Island-based franchiser of garage systems, offers another type of garage scheme. The company installs custom-designed floors, cabinets, and shelves in an effort to transform garages into usable, flexible space. Slotted wall-storage panels that look a bit like retail-store displays allow you to hang up just about anything you can imagine. Many homeowners who use wall systems combine them with closed cabinetry to hide the less-presentable items. A company like GarageTek can remodel a two-car garage measuring twenty by twenty feet in just one or two days. The folks at Whirlpool have joined in this burgeoning consumer demand for garage storage systems, as well. Its line, called Gladiator GarageWorks, is another alterative to the traditional peg-board scheme, offering component panels or slot-full wall systems to reclaim valuable floor space. The company offers a free online tool called the Blueprint Estimator that allows you to design your own modular garage system. Visit *www.gladiatorgw.com* for details.

If you live in a four-season climate, you'll probably want to rearrange your garage at least once or twice a year. Sure, it entails a bit of extra work, but, on the bright side, it also gives you additional opportunities to give your gear another once- or twice-over and determine what's worth keeping around. If you store your patio furniture inside for the winter, the ceiling rafters are an ideal place. Open, adjustable rafter shelves can be attached to the roof truss of your garage. Not only that, they can handle car seats, camping gear, and ski equipment, among other things, without getting in the way of your parked vehicles. If your garage is tall enough, you might even think about constructing a storage loft area using a bunk bed–style ladder to access it.

Word to the Wise

There are two main types of garage doors. A swing-up or tilt model is made of a single panel that pivots out and upward. Sectional roll-up doors, which are more expensive, are constructed of several sections that are hinged together and mounted onto a track with rollers.

Consider elevated platforms that lower to the ground for a motorcycle, scooter, snow blower, or lawn mower. A lift-and-pulley system is a useful floor-clearing device to get your bicycles out of the line of foot traffic. Another option is to mount bikes flush to the wall and add an additional rack for helmets and other accessories. If you're the tool-shy type, try an adjustable-tension design rack that can be secured to the walls or ceiling without any hardware or having to make any holes.

High Mileage

There's never been a better time to get your garage into shape. Sales of garage storage products grew an astounding 40 percent in just five years, which means there are plenty of solutions on the market available to tailor a system to your lifestyle. How dramatic do you want to get? Do you prefer taking a do-it-yourself approach? Or would you rather hire a professional garage-makeover company? Your wallet, habits, and the importance you place on your garage's resemblance to a multifunctional new-car showroom will dictate your answer.

Whatever approach you take, as you begin to get the clutter organized and under control in your garage, you'll begin to experience the benefits. Although you may not often realize how much the clutter kept in your garage drains your energy, when you begin to clear it out, you'll feel as if you have a larger home. Your cars will be happier if they can park there (and so will you, come winter mornings). You'll also save money when your supplies are easy to access because you won't accidentally purchase things you already own. Who knows—by making your garage orderly and finding safer ways to store the dangerous items, you could even save a life. Just as we never really know how much clutter costs us, it is also hard to know, until we begin to tackle it, how much can be gained by bringing order to these often-overlooked spaces.

Chapter 17
The Great Outdoors

SOMETIMES, CLUTTER SPILLS OUT OF THE HOME AND INTO THE OUT-SIDE SPACE. Decks, patios, and sheds often need attention to become and remain useful and attractive. As you bring order to your yard, you have an opportunity to create a serene refuge for your family—a place for play, peace, and entertaining. This chapter offers helpful information on how to fulfill the true potential of your outdoor space.

Your Deck and Patio

Deck and patio space is often at a premium, so you'll want to be careful about how you arrange the space. You'll want to make sure that any furniture you select is not too large for the existing space, and if you often have guests, you'll want to be able to add seating should the need arise. Invest in high-quality furniture because deck furniture will be exposed to the elements (even if you store it inside during the winters). Try to buy top-quality items at the end of the season when they're all on sale, or at outlet stores from manufacturers you trust. If you visit an outlet store at the end of the season, you could save as much as 70 percent on your purchase. You'll get quality furniture that will last for years to come, but you'll pay a fraction of the original cost.

Also, think in terms of comfort. If you love to sit outside and read or you'll be spending hours out there watching your kids, you'll never regret purchasing a chair that is as comfortable as your inside furniture. Many stores sell deck chairs with ottomans that have large, durable, washable weatherproof cushions that wear well over time. Investing in high-quality cushions will let you kick back and enjoy the outdoors.

One of the best ways to keep your deck and patio uncluttered is to store any items that you aren't currently using. Frequently purge items the moment they lose their value—cracked pots need not be fixed, bent rakes will do you no good in the fall. Take a ruthless approach to keeping broken things out of your yard, and you'll be better able to appreciate the beauty that thrives there. When plants die (as they inevitably will), take care of them promptly instead of watching their slow disintegration on your porch. This can be depressing for you and can compromise the beauty and freshness of your outdoor space.

Word to the Wise

You'll want to bring cushions in to store them for the winter, but make sure that they have been cleaned and completely dried before you tuck them away. Otherwise, stains will set and mold might even intrude, making the cushions unusable. Also, be sure to store cushions in an area that is free from mold and humidity.

Be sure to keep lawn implements in a shed or garage instead of right on the limited patio/porch space. Also, if space is tight, you might use window boxes or plant boxes along the perimeter of the porch so that you don't use up valuable space on your porch.

Consider purchasing hardy wood furnishings (benches and the like) that can provide storage on your deck. These can often be found with wheels on the bottom, which will dramatically increase their function—should you have company over, you can easily rearrange these items to make your guests comfortable.

Kidding Around

A yard can be a great place for little feet and little minds to explore. Children who play outside have the opportunity for much-needed unstructured free play, while those who sit inside in front of the television are more likely to struggle with obesity.

Although having a yard is great for families with small children, these green spaces can present many challenges, especially if you've accumulated more playthings than your children know how to use. Be aggressive about purging outdoor toys when they are rarely used, and place the burden of the work on your children's shoulders. You might purchase a small wagon so that your children can easily transport their own toys outside. After an afternoon of play, make sure that your children load up the wagon and return the toys to their inside home.

If you want to keep toys in the yard, you can use a sturdy plastic toy chest that can be kept on the deck. A large plastic garbage bin can serve as great storage for bats, balls, and other sports equipment. To reduce the possibility of a yard littered with plastic toys (and kids who are too overwhelmed by the sheer number of toys to pick them up themselves), you can limit the number of toys allowed in the yard at any one time (choose a number that works for your family, such as five or ten).

You might also want to rotate toys that are kept in the bin. Many times, if toy bins are too overstuffed, kids won't remember what toys they have. Toys are quickly outgrown, and some toys never capture a kid's interest. If you purge these items, your child will be better able to see what he has. Not only will the child play more with the toys he does have, but he'll also be more likely to participate in cleanup.

In terms of play equipment in the yard—gym equipment, plastic play-houses, and the like—take note of how often they are used. If you begin to sense that your children are no longer enjoying them, look for another home for these items. These kinds of things tend to be bulky, heavy, and difficult to move. Simplify your life (and beautify your yard) by getting rid of as many of these items as you (and your children) can let go of.

Make sure that all of this equipment is still safe for use. When these items begin to break down and become warped, get rid of them quickly to protect your children's safety. Because these items are often used for climbing, jumping, and other energetic activity, you'll want to be sure that they are structurally sound. Also check with the manufacturer about appropriate ages and weights. As soon as children become too large or old, consider passing the items on to smaller children in the neighborhood.

Watch Out!

If your children haven't used the play equipment in the backyard for several months, ask them why. Perhaps they've begun to outgrow the items or bugs have gotten into them. Playhouses can quickly become havens for insects and sandboxes can become litter boxes for cats. Once you uncover the problem, you can remedy the situation or get rid of the equipment.

Fire Up the Grill

The position of your grill is extremely important. If it is too close to your home or stored on a wood porch, it could present a fire hazard. You'll also want to keep it several feet away from your outside dining or sitting area. Before purchasing a grill, think about how often you will use it and where it will be stored. If you'll only use it occasionally, your best bet is probably a grill that is on wheels and can be stored in a shed or garage.

Purchasing a grill can be a confusing task because there are so many options available. Some are natural-gas powered, while others use propane gas or charcoal. Also, to lengthen the life of charcoal or smoking chips, keep them dry and raised.

The Bottom Line

Propane gas is a fire hazard. Do not store propane tanks in your home. A shed is a better option. If storage of flammable materials is a problem, you might want a gas grill that can be installed on your deck and connected to your home's gas supply. With a direct gas line, you can fire up the grill instantly without charcoal or propane.

If you'll be grilling near children, take extra caution with matches, lighter fluid, and all flammable materials. Warn children that the grill will remain extremely hot for a long time after use. Grill tools are also often sharp and dangerous, so these should be carefully tucked away after use.

You can purchase a small, lockable storage chest to keep on your deck or patio. Inside, you can store items such as citronella candles, grilling utensils, matches, and other items. If you store anything flammable in this chest, make sure to keep all cloth products and sporting equipment in another area.

Storage Sheds

It you have several bulky items that you want to keep close to your yard, consider purchasing an outdoor storage shed. An outdoor storage shed is ideal for housing a lawn mower, rakes, garden hoses, sprinklers, shovels, fertilizers, and other garden tools. These small sheds are built to withstand the elements and to provide non–climate-controlled storage inside.

One of the things to keep in mind when planning for a shed is that many communities have regulations pertaining to sheds. These requirements concern such details as where a shed can and can't be located, its size, and possibly its appearance.

As you plan for a shed, think in terms of aesthetics as well as function. Sheds can be purchased in natural woods, such as cedar, which is rot-resistant (although it does require maintenance). Some materials, such as steel, are prone to rust, while aluminum is far more durable. Likewise, if you choose to purchase a shed with vinyl siding, make sure that you invest in a high-quality product so that the siding will not warp over time.

Before purchasing a shed, you'll need to answer the following questions:

- What elements and other conditions will your shed be exposed to?
- What will you be storing in your shed?
- Do the contents of your shed need to be kept in a water-free environment?
- Does the shed need to be temperature controlled?
- Will the shed require electricity?
- Based on what you need to store, how large must the shed be?
- Where on your property will the shed be installed?

Storage sheds are available in a variety of shapes, sizes, and orientations: horizontal or vertical, top or front-loading, with lifting or sliding roofs. They are generally simple to assemble and require little or no maintenance. The greatest challenge they might pose (like your garage) is the challenge of keeping the items within them organized. It can be tempting, with any space that is rarely seen, to let clutter accumulate and chaos reign. If you know that you tend to toss random items into your closets inside the house, you might want to avoid purchasing a shed, as it could present further temptations to you.

Word to the Wise

Sheds can be placed on several different types of foundations. A shed can be placed on a 3- to 4-inch bed of crushed stone. If the site is soft or you want protection from frost, use a pier foundation with pressure-treated columns on concrete footings. Sheds can also be placed on concrete or stone patios.

Because your shed is a semi-permanent structure, you'll want to take care when choosing a location for it. It must be level, and you want to be sure that the ground around the shed drains properly so that you do not flood your shed. Also, keep in mind that any door on a shed should have adequate clearance for storing your largest items, such as a lawn mower.

Tooling Around

Start by whittling your lawn and garden equipment down to what you really need and what actually works, then start organizing! Begin by breaking your tools down into categories such as:

- Manual tools, such as rakes and shovels

- Pots and statuaries

- Chemicals

- Seeds, bulbs, and other small items

- Soil, chips, birdseed, and any other materials that come in oversized bulky bags

- Large equipment, like lawn mowers and wheelbarrows

Here's the game plan. Think about how you're going to access something, not just about putting it away. Store the tools and products you use most in the front for easy in-and-out access. Little-used ones go in the back. However, seasonality will play a part. Figure on doing some rearranging at least twice a year. Snowblowers and snow shovels go to the head of the line in winter, until the lawn mower and weed whacker come out in spring.

The Bottom Line

Organic gardening is a method that uses only materials derived from living things, such as compost and manure, for fertilization and pest control. In contrast to conventional gardening, the organic approach uses no synthetic chemicals at all.

For rakes, shovels, hoes, outdoor brooms, and other long-handled tools, use nails, hooks, or handle grippers to hang them on the wall, heads up, instead of leaning them precariously against the wall, where they could become a tripping hazard. Organize small hand tools all together in such a way to let you easily grab and go. Pegboards will do the trick for tools as well as for small-handled pails. Trestles also make great utility posts. Another option for small items is to store them in convenient tote kits or hard cases, which will protect them from the elements.

Garden tools work better if they're in tip-top shape. Without proper maintenance, they can easily become caked with dirt and rendered useless. Unplug power tools before performing any maintenance or repairs. When filing or sharpening blades, be sure to wear safety goggles and leather gloves.

Hang ladders and wheelbarrows on U-hooks secured into the ceiling or on a wall using heavy-duty brackets. Get out-of-season lawn furniture out of the way by stowing it in the rafters of the garage. Another practical option is a mobile cart. For larger tools, like rakes and shovels, along with heavy-to-lug sacks of soil, rolling carts give you storage and freedom to roam throughout your property.

Plants and Planters

Nestle pots together to save space, using padding in between to prevent scratches. Stack plastic pots together and saucers separately. Terracotta pots can swell and crack, so it's best to lie them on their sides in a wood carton. Keep them in an area away from traffic flow. Be sure to bring pots made of clay or other fragile material inside for the winter. If you live in a cold-weather climate, you probably already know that some containers don't hold up to subfreezing temperatures. Be sure to clean and dry them thoroughly before storing to prevent disease.

Coil hoses and hang them on L-shaped hooks on the wall when off-duty for the season. Large, wide-mouthed planter containers also make handy homes for garden and soaking hoses. To avoid the "crazy coiling" syndrome altogether, buy a mobile hose cart that goes in the garage or shed in winter and rolls out and hooks up to your outdoor faucet in summer.

An Organized Inquiry

What's the best way to store bulbs for the winter? After the season, dig up bulbs, brush off soil, and let them air dry to prevent rotting. Then store them in a bag or box with peat moss in a cool, dry place. Check them periodically for signs of insects, rot, or damage. If you spot any rot, cut away the affected section. And be sure to label the bulbs so you know what you'll be planting down the road.

When storing large bags of mulch, peat, lime, and topsoil, make sure you keep them on low shelves that can sustain the weight. If you buy in bulk, try to consolidate whenever possible. It's both a matter of organization and inventory tracking. You'll know exactly what you have on hand. There's nothing more frustrating than digging into what you think is a large bag of fertilizer only to discover it's almost empty. Transfer contents of big, heavy bags into smaller, lidded containers to prevent spills. Check your local garden center or department store for durable, lightweight containers that can accommodate any size or quantity. Consider purchasing a tray with multiple drawers to store small items such as seed packets, bulbs, and work gloves.

Cultivate Delight

Whatever you choose to do with your own little patch of green, keep in mind that this space allows you the opportunity to create sensory delight—you can grow edibles here, nurture lovely flowers, or create a serene retreat to relax in at the end of the day. The order you bring to the outside of your home need not be as elaborate as the order you seek to cultivate inside your home, but it can certainly be nourishing to your soul and body. If you are intentional about making your yard a place that is both healthy and beautiful, you will bless your neighbors and yourself. There are millions of ways to do this in your yard. Experiment with different ideas until you're able to create the green space you desire. And whatever you do, cherish the time spent in your yard. Don't stress yourself out by looking at a green lawn marred by rusted or rusting tools or toys strewn about the yard. Millions of people in urban areas around the world would relish the opportunity to have a small patch of green to call their own—a place for solitude, reflection, and transformation. As Diane Ackerman writes, "Just cultivate delight. Enjoy the sensory pleasures of the garden. That's number one." If you can cultivate delight, the rest will fall into place.

part 6

special occasions

EVERYBODY LOVES TO ENTERTAIN, but people so often find themselves buried beneath the trappings of holidays, birthdays, and other special occasions. After all, where are you going to store that ten-foot Santa Claus in August? Where are you going to put the spare china that only sees the light of day on Thanksgiving?

Ensuring that serving platters and decorations don't fall prey to disorganization is difficult for even the most seasoned host, but the following chapters are here to help you find a home for both your Christmas stockings and your crystal. After all, what good is having an organized home if you can't share it with your friends and family?

Chapter 18

Organized Entertaining

SOME ASPIRE TO BE THE HOST WITH THE MOST. Others hope to be the host with the least—the least anxiety and the least disorganization, that is. It comes naturally to a few. You know who they are. In this chapter, you'll get tips, strategies, and a game plan that will help you get the party started. Learn the tricks for being a cool, calm, and collected host. You can actually boost expectations by scaling back and simplifying. Bring on the guests.

The Wrong Stuff

There's the aunt who's always first in line to host every holiday dinner; the friend with the Type A personality who sends out "save the date" reminders a season early; the rah-rah neighbor who coordinates the annual block party down to the tiniest of details. Yet what may look effortless on the outside is actually the culmination of good planning and proper timing. If these enthusiastic party planners always seem to have their act together, it's because they organize, utilize, and improvise.

Watch Out!

Improper cooling of foods can cause illnesses. Avoid covering or stacking foods during the initial cooling stages. It prevents the heat from escaping. And don't leave cooked foods at room temperature for more than two hours. If you're not going to be digging into the goodies for a couple of days, put them in the freezer and stick a label on them identifying the dish and the date.

Where do you fall on the organization scale? You're hosting a party. It's ten o'clock. The doorbell rings. The first guests are here. Are you:

A. Still in your sweatpants and bedroom slippers?

B. Wondering where the good table linen is?

C. Searching for recipes for the evening's menu?

D. All of the above?

If your own soirees are more of an exercise in frustration than fun, it's time to go back to basics. For one thing, do you have too much of the wrong stuff taking up unnecessary space in your closets and cabinets? Take a run through this checklist and see how many of these situations apply:

- Mismatched glasses and dishes; two of this, three of that, but not a complete set in the bunch

- Lots of gadgets, appliances, and dishes that serve a single niche role—think olive dishes, caviar spoons, and frittata grills

- Recipes strewn about in cookbooks, notebooks, and kitchen drawers, with no logical filing system to keep them in order

- Tablecloths, placemats, and napkins that match the décor . . . of your last home

- Creased wrapping paper rolls and bags of crushed bows and ribbons

- Decorations celebrating long-ago milestones, like "Congratulations, Graduate!" napkins and "Happy 40th Birthday" paper cups

- Sets and serving pieces for every individual holiday and occasion

These are some sure signs that the countdown to each social gathering is fraught with inefficiency and stress.

The Bottom Line

In the publishing world, cookbooks have long been perennial favorites. One of the most successful cookbooks of all time was first published in 1896, when a woman by the name of Fannie Merritt Farmer took on the editorship of the Boston Cooking-School Cook Book. Farmer was the first to standardize the methods and measurements of her recipes, thereby assuring chefs a reliable outcome.

The other roadblock is lacking a sensible storage strategy for your special occasion items. Are the things you need for entertaining scattered in rooms throughout the house? Take Annie, a sometimes-happy hostess. She loves having her friends and family over for brunches and dinner parties but lacks a sane system for housing her partyware. She described preparations for one recent anniversary dinner that involved gathering special baking pans from a utility cabinet in the basement, table linens from a hall closet, and special china from the attic. And those were only the things whose location she could actually remember. She never did find the napkin rings.

Stock and Trade

Take stock of the items you cart out for special occasions and especially those you leave behind. They're the biggest space wasters of all. Throw out anything that's warped, chipped, broken, or stained, tempting through it may be to hold on to the tablecloth with the red wine stain you try to hide under the candlestick holder.

Some people like to mix and match different sets of plates or glasses if they don't have full sets, but if that's not your style, then move them out of your home and down to the neighborhood thrift shop or charity organization. Are you overstocked with more cake platters than a bakery and more cheese plates than a French bistro? Don't stockpile more items than you can reasonably expect to use. Find another home for the excess.

Word to the Wise

Outdoor entertainment can keep a party going. Want to watch the big game on an HDTV while firing up the grill? Easily done. These days, outdoor home theaters are as elaborate as the state-of-the-art systems homeowners have in their media rooms. Weatherproof video systems can be hung from a valence or designed to pop up from the landscaping.

Often, homeowners are inundated with trays, platters, and serving dishes through no fault of their own. They're the recipients of dozens of anniversary, birthday, Christmas, and hostess gifts received over the years. Discard them? Heaven forbid. What will Aunt Lena think if her candy dish isn't prominently displayed? Take an inventory to see how many of these types of items you have squirreled away in your home. If it's more than a few, it's time to bite the bullet and devise an exit strategy. You do your generous gift-givers no favors by holding onto a present you never display or use.

Are you a "phase" chef? You know, someone who latches onto a specialty for a while and then buys up everything in sight to feed the fix? Four years ago it was your tart-jellyroll-cupcake baking phase, and you've still got every pan to prove it. But now that you've moved onto

ORGANIZED ENTERTAINING

roasts for family fetes, the old baking gear has attained relic status in your cupboards. Clear them out and pass them on.

Watch Out!

Attend to spills and stains right away. The longer they sit, the less chance you'll have of 100 percent success. Two of the biggest offenders are candle wax and red wine. To remove candle wax from a tablecloth, harden the wax using ice cubes, and scrape it off with a dull knife. For wine stains, act fast. Pour salt onto the stain, then blot the tablecloth with cold water. Wipe up water, too, especially on hardwoods.

Do you have items too good to toss but too much trouble to use? Think about your beautiful silver candlestick holders. The idea of all that polishing has you running straight for the low-maintenance crystal pair instead. Then there's the waffle iron, when the frozen toaster kind will do just fine. And how about the pasta machine when your family enjoys the good old reliable store-bought brands? These are the kinds of items that sound good in theory but that fall short when it comes to the realities of our time-constrained days. If you can't remember the last time you used it, move it out. Quite often we don't even realize how much of this special-occasion stuff we have because we rarely go in search of it. One woman had a fondue set. It was used exactly one time for company, but it took up the better part of a cabinet shelf for years on end. She just couldn't bring herself to get rid of something that was in "like-new" condition.

Rites and Wrongs

What about all the pretty heirloom dishes you hold on to out of guilt? It's a huge problem, according to Misha Keefe, an organizing guru. She says the guilt factor when doing any kind of purge of personal items is enormous.

Keefe suggests passing on sentimental items to other family members. It might be more appropriate to their tastes or suitable for their needs; yet at the same time, you're still keeping it within the family. Not practical? If you inherited, say, your grandmother's china set and it's just sitting crated up in the basement, you're not doing her memory any honor by leaving it there. Take out one or two pieces and showcase them on a shelf. Then sell the rest. The key is detaching the sentimental value from the individual associated with it.

Word to the Wise

Mood lighting is one of the most undervalued elements of home entertaining. Marry the lighting to the task or tasks at hand. Use soft lights for an intimate dinner party and brighter lights for large-scale entertaining. For extra fun any time of year, snake a string of little white Christmas lights along the top of an entertainment unit or wrap the string around a large potted plant.

For years, Jessica had an ornate gold-trimmed cake platter a favorite cousin had given her just sitting in bubble wrap in her basement. As pretty as the platter was, it just didn't go with any of Jessica's décor. Finally—and reluctantly—she decided to sell it at a yard sale. Her guilt was palpable as potential customers neared. But the feeling instantly disappeared when a browser spotted the plate and became ecstatic over her discovery. As the sale transpired, Jessica realized her cousin's gift would be more cherished in another home.

Task Masters

The quantity of entertaining paraphernalia should have some relationship to the number of barbeques, bashes, and dinner parties you throw. If it's not a lot, reduce, reduce, reduce! Items reserved for infrequent guests shouldn't dominate, particularly at the expense of your everyday needs.

Need it? Yes. But do you have to own it? Not necessarily. Think twice about whether owning a twenty-four-cup coffee urn is necessary for that once-a-year book club meeting you host. One family of non–coffee drinkers simply buys "boxes" of java from their local doughnut shop whenever the need arises, instead of having a coffeemaker dominating a shelf year-round.

You can always borrow specialty cookware from friends, neighbors, and relatives. One woman who lives in a condo development borrows extra folding chairs from her development's clubhouse every year for her Passover seder. Rent appliances, china, chairs, and linens and more from party supply shops. You'd be surprised at the wide range of loaners available these days, everything from chafing dishes and chocolate fountains to barbecue grills and punchbowls. Of course, using paper plates and plastic cups will free up your storage space. If, however, the idea of throwaway place settings weighs on your conscience, there are companies that make disposable flatware and plates out of organic materials.

An Organized Inquiry

How can I throw an environmentally friendly party? Print invitations on recycled paper or tree-free materials such as hemp, organic cotton, or banana stalks. Instead of cut flowers, use a potted plant as a centerpiece that can be replanted later. For outdoor affairs, battle mosquitoes with fans and citronella candles instead of pesticide sprays. Find out about donating leftovers to a neighborhood food pantry or soup kitchen.

Simplify your tableware with fewer specialty items and more versatile ones that can serve a myriad of functions. The marketplace is flooded with items designed for niche purposes. Guess who benefits?

Do you really need turkey-decorated dishes that are just used for a single Thanksgiving Day meal? Or red, white, and blue drinking glasses for Independence Day? When it comes to dishes and plates, go the generic route. Instead of cartons full of entertaining pieces for every special occasion, maintain a set of adaptable dishes and multipurpose platters you can use over and over. But don't mistake basic for boring. Dress them up with seasonal herbs, garnishes, and even edible flowers.

If you insist on holding on to your holiday-theme dishes, bowls, and mugs, realize you'll need to take extra steps to be more organized because of them. Purchase large plastic tubs, separate them by holiday or occasion, and clearly label them: kids' birthdays, Valentine's Day decorations, New Year's Eve, etc.

In the case of storage tubs, bigger is better. If you store items in a lot of little containers, you'll have more difficulty keeping track of all you've got, and they're more likely to wind up strewn in various closets and cabinets throughout your home.

Institute a system that flows naturally with your lifestyle by reconfiguring your storage to better fit your day-to-day requirements. For instance, if you regularly eat meals in your dining room, don't fill your china cabinet drawers with table linens that are used only on rare occasions for company. Make it work to suit your needs. See to it that the drawers house your everyday place settings. Your storage plan should be straightforward and intuitive. The less you use a given item, the farther it should be from your daily realm.

Group like items together. Keep all decorating items together, like garnishing tools and cake decorating tips. Store special baking items all in one spot. Do the same with "for-company-only" utensils and serving dishes.

Take the stress out of company cleanups. Line casserole dishes and pans with aluminum foil and baking trays with parchment paper. It's an easy way to say goodbye to caked-on grease and stubborn stains. Out of baking dishes? Use disposable aluminum trays, available at the supermarket, instead.

Serves You Right

Any reason for a celebration will do: birthdays, holidays, anniversaries, graduations. Do more with less. Use snack tables that have removable tops that can also be used as serving trays. Double-handled "gathering" baskets, made originally for gathering flowers from the garden, are ideal to hold breads or a smattering of little appetizer plates that can then easily be passed around from guest to guest. Some baskets are long enough and shallow enough to be used to hold place settings and napkins if you're hosting a buffet. Think vertically by using tiered plate holders that take up minimal table space with their elfin footprints.

The Bottom Line

Ninety percent of households in the United States buy greeting cards, purchasing an average of thirty-five cards a year, according to the greeting card industry. With cards ranging from 50 cents to $10, Americans generate more than $7.5 billion in retail sales every year. Who's doing most of the buying? Women. They purchase more than 80 percent of all greeting cards.

Have a table for six with no leaf expansion capabilities? No problem. If you're planning dinner for eight or ten, cut a sheet of plywood to size, throw on a tablecloth and you've got a custom table instantly proportioned for your affair.

Instead of buying more, simply reinvent. Here's how:

- Use elegant martini glasses to serve nuts or olives.

- Serve breadsticks in tall, slender parfait glasses.

- Repurpose pretty soup bowls for salsa and spreads.

- Carve out breads, tomatoes, and peppers to use as dip holders.

- Serve cheeses on wooden cutting boards.

- Display fresh flowers in pretty water pitchers.

Rethinking your furniture configuration is an often-overlooked aspect of entertaining. Make sure there are clear paths between rooms for guests to wander. Plant stands, chairs, statues, and other decorative pieces can wind up obstructing thresholds and cause traffic roadblocks.

Crystal-Clear Solutions

China, crystal, and fragile antique serving pieces deserve TLC, attention, and special storage consideration. If you house china in a cabinet, make sure to put felt pads or other cushioning material between layers to prevent scratches and chips. Stack cups no more than two high to avoid tumbling. Hanging them from small hooks is even better. If your china is behind closed doors, cushioned storage pouches will keep the pieces protected and dust-free. And don't forget the padded layers. Should you lose a piece in an accident, there's hope. The International Association of Dinnerware Matchers (www.iadm.com) is a group of independent dealers that can help you locate hard-to-find and even discontinued china, crystal, and flatware pieces.

Crystal and other delicate glassware should be stored stem-side down so there's no undue pressure on the rim. Keep a little "breathing" space between the glasses to head off accidental chipping. If possible, it's always a good idea to store fragile dishware in a cabinet that's segregated from your everyday, heavily used dishes so it doesn't accidentally get tussled about.

Watch Out!

Not everything should go in the dishwasher. Wash delicate crystal and china by hand, especially those that are antique or have hand-painting or metal trim. When hand washing, put a rubber pad at the bottom of the sink as a cushion for extra protection. Dry immediately so you can put items away—and out of harm's way.

Food for Thought

When the next gathering comes around, you'll be more attentive to your guests if you economize your actions and scale down your party gear. Get rid of anything that's not pulling its weight. Sure, it's nice to have special dishes and accessories for company or to celebrate a holiday—it sets the day apart—but you never want so many that they intrude on the storage capabilities of your everyday things. Reframe how you think about those things. Separate the need-to-haves from the nice-to-haves.

Can't remember when you used it last? Lose it—fast. Keeping rarely utilized items or multiple sets of dishes, appliances, platters, and more is plain uneconomical and inefficient, even some items that hold sentimental value. There are better ways to pay tribute to a memory than keeping something boxed up in bubble wrap. Disassociate the thing from the person who gave it to you.

Hang on to host-and-hostess helpers that are most versatile, the accessories that will take you from season to season and celebration to celebration. The simple act of decluttering will calm you down and make time work in your favor.

Chapter 19

Celebrate Harmonious Holidays

DECK THE HALLS . . . IF YOU CAN FIND THE DECORATIONS, that is. Christmas, Thanksgiving Day, Halloween—whatever the holiday, the celebration's not quite complete without all the trimmings to go along with it: the table settings, the specially designed baking dishes, and the indoor and outdoor ornamentations. Keep it all neatly under wraps with tailor-made stowaway solutions guaranteed to keep your holidays jolly.

Christmas Past and Presents

No matter how much you look forward to a holiday celebration, there's always a certain amount of stress and anxiety involved. Cleaning, shopping, decorating, sprucing up, hosting. The to-do lists are ever growing. What's more, they seem to start earlier every year. The proof? Before you can say "trick or treat," the shopping malls are already adorned in their jingle-bell finery. Before you can wish your neighbor a Happy New Year, the aroma of Valentine's Day chocolate truffles is wafting through the candy aisles. You might not be able to control the stepped-up timetable of the retail industry, but you can reduce some of the "holidaze" while increasing the enjoyment quotient by getting organized.

The Bottom Line

In the early nineteenth century, the American ambassador to Mexico, Joe Poinsett, brought home a plant that ultimately came to be named after him, the poinsettia. Less than a century later, the beautiful red and green poinsettia has become a widespread symbol of Christmas.

In the average home, a large chunk of closet, attic, and basement space is given over to holiday gear, and it just keeps growing. What might have been a few pretty ornaments, a tree stand, skirt, and some twinkling lights in the old days has now mushroomed into a full-blown North Pole spectacle. And that's just for Christmas. Move over, Santa. Cupid, the Easter Bunny, and the Great Pumpkin are approaching fast. Decorating the home has become a four-season sport.

Halloween is second only to Christmas as the biggest decorating holiday of the year. Some 60 percent of consumers go in for Halloween decoration purchases. Ghosts, goblins, scarecrows, black cats, and jack 'o lanterns of every size turn homes and gardens into funhouse displays. Trick-or-treating might be for the young, but Halloween is being increasingly embraced by the young at heart, and they're the ones pulling out all the stops.

It's a good thing for America's closets that other big holidays like Valentine's Day, Mother's Day, Father's Day, and Thanksgiving, as well as many religious holidays like Chanukah, Passover, and Easter, are centered on more transitory priorities such as food, flowers, and greeting cards. Jelly beans and chocolate bunnies may be responsible for piling on the pounds, but thankfully they don't create storage woes.

Christmas Countdown

There's always great anticipation to the start of every holiday season, a chance to gift-wrap your home in lights and make it a warm and welcoming place for friends and family to drop by.

Cheryl, a holistic health practitioner from Long Island, says her parents always made her childhood home a winter wonderland and, as an adult, she's happy to follow suit. But it isn't out of obligation. It just feels so good. Each silver candelabra, carved Santa statuette, and satin stocking has its own specialness, Cheryl says, and that's why every Christmas her home feels like a huge warm hug. The very act of decorating, adds her boyfriend Greg, is a constant that runs throughout the season. Among Greg's own traditions is wrapping gifts to a Robert Goulet CD soundtrack. It's a ritual Greg started thirty years ago—only then he was listening to the same recording on an LP.

Introduce rituals into your decorating activities to take out some of the drudge work. Put on a seasonal CD or a favorite holiday movie as a backdrop, like *White Christmas*, *It's a Wonderful Life*, or *Holiday Inn*. And don't put too much pressure on yourself by trying to decorate the whole house in a single day. Deck your halls over the course of a few days or even weeks so you don't feel overwhelmed. The measured pace will show in the details of your labor.

Watch Out!

If you have toddlers or pets that love to poke around the Christmas tree, decorate it with shatterproof ornaments. Although they look like glass, the ornaments are unbreakable because they're actually made of reflective resin. Any danger is averted, and you don't have to sacrifice style.

It's the lead-up to Christmas that leaves so many people unraveled. The picture-perfect family we imagine decorating the tree, placing candles in the windows and a wreath lovingly on the door—singing carols all the while—is the stuff of Hollywood fiction. Instead of "Ho-ho-ho," the exclamations are usually unprintable, and not very family-friendly. The reason for that can be directly traced to what happened at the end of the previous season. If last winter's cleanup ended with a get-it-over-with-it attitude once the festivities died down, you've set yourself up for a frustrating kick-off to another Christmas. Sloppy habits always come back to haunt you.

This year, plan on spending some extra time before and after the holidays reorganizing your Christmas wares. You'll shave off time and put the brakes on endless searches. It's guaranteed to make the next season brighter. Have an idea of what you want to do before you begin. You can always rearrange things later on.

Season Opener

Take out all your holiday items, especially the ones you haven't used in years. Look carefully through your closets and cabinets. Things like winter-plaid table linens, holly-decorated ice buckets, and berry centerpieces may be strewn in the far reaches of your home. One family rediscovered a box of holiday linens left ages ago in a storage alley in the attic only after embarking on an insulation project. Haul all your items to one central area, kind of like a Santa's workshop, for examining and sorting. Throw out any items that are chipped, faded, or damaged.

What you liked and how you decorated years ago might not match your tastes anymore. Even Christmas decorations go out of style. Instead of ignoring the things you're no longer interested in and letting them waste storage space, get rid of them. Donate them to a thrift shop to brighten someone else's home for the holidays, to a church, or to an individual just starting out in her own apartment.

If you have small decorative items too pretty to throw out, use them to dress up your gift-wrapping or greeting cards.

Consider selling valuable pieces you no longer have a use for either online or through a classified ad. Many Christmas villages and ornaments are highly collectible. One seasonal fan whose friends dub him Father Christmas sells off old pieces each year so he can continue adding new ones to his collection without clogging up storage space in his home.

Word to the Wise

Before buying those baking molds, specialty appliances, and cookie cutters you use only once a year, see if you can borrow what you need from a friend or neighbor. You can even start a new tradition of hosting a kitchen swap or organizing a lending library of seasonal goods that will save everyone money while giving you a good excuse to get together with pals.

Yuletide Wrap-Up

It's December 26. The presents are all unwrapped, the annual New Year's weight-loss resolution is just days away, and the houseful of Christmas paraphernalia is staring at you, waiting to be put away for another year. Before the packing begins, think strategically.

Get out a notebook and create a holiday organizer. In it you can do all these things:

- Keep tabs on presents bought and received. It'll prevent you from buying Aunt Martha yet another set of pajamas and dish towels next year.

- Note food preparations and what dishes you've made for company. What were the hits? What were the misses? And who was allergic to what?

- Inventory your holiday decorations. When next season rolls around, you'll know exactly what you've got. No chance you'll buy another set of silver snowflake napkin-holders by accident.

- Track your greeting card distribution: the people you sent cards, and those whose cards you received. One mom even saves a sample of the Chanukah picture postcards of her family she sends out each year as a special holiday keepsake.

When undecorating, use color-coded storage containers so you can spot holiday stash more easily. Red and green will stand out from your standard storage tubs. Use orange and black for Halloween, brown for Thanksgiving, red for Valentine's Day, and so on. If you enlist personal elves to assist you with the task, your helpers will always know exactly just what boxes to reach for.

Label your containers clearly and be as specific as possible. Don't just write "Christmas." Jot down exactly what Christmas items are inside like "Baking dishes" or "Santa suit."

Avoid packing holiday candles away in attics. The heat will warp them. Find a cool area instead.

Watch Out!

If you save leftover holiday cards to use the following season or take advantage of after-Christmas sales to enjoy half-price card savings, store them in an area of your home that won't subject them to extreme temperatures or high humidity. One December, a woman discovered, much to her distress, that her stash of cards purchased the prior season was ruined because humidity had sealed the envelopes shut.

Have a rationale behind your storage approach to make subsequent set-ups a no-brainer. One strategy is to pack like items together. For instance, have all your lights in one box, all decorative figurines in another, and tree skirt, stand, and floor protector in a third. Another method is to pack by room. Somehow we seem to suffer amnesia from one year to the next. Where does the six-foot string of twinkle lights go again? In what room does the ceramic tabletop tree belong? That won't happen next year if you make your containers room-specific. That way all objects that go in the dining room, say, are together, and all outdoor objects are in another container. Go one step further. Attach little notes to each applicable piece before you tuck it away for the season reminding you where in the room it goes. If the white lights are designated for the bay window and the fuzzy snowman on the fireplace mantel, take an extra moment to note it.

The Bottom Line

Santa Claus is believed to be inspired by a bishop who lived in the fourth century named Saint Nicholas of Myra, now located in modern Turkey. The bishop was remembered for his generosity.

There are some items you may need to get to first, before the heavy artillery of decorations comes out. Place these in the most accessible areas, where they'll be easy to grab. Some people like getting an early jump on their baking, gift-wrapping, or card-writing, for instance.

Before you pack away ornaments, remove hooks to prevent scratches and mars.

If you have an artificial tree and tend to decorate it the same way year after year—and you have the room—you don't necessarily have to undecorate it at the end of the season. Throw a big plastic bag or tarp over it, and it'll be set up and ready to go next December. It's definitely the way to go for tabletop-size trees. The same thing goes with artificial wreaths, centerpieces, and garlands.

Going natural will really cut down on your storage needs. Buy a live tree and fresh greenery, and you won't have to think about off-season storage at all. Some communities even have programs in which trees are collected after Christmas and then chopped up into mulch, which is then offered free to residents. In New York City, for example, residents can drop off their trees and wreaths during "Mulchfest" at selected parks.

Check with your local municipality to see if there's a similar program in your neighborhood.

Tailor-Made Solutions

Many Christmas items are oddly shaped or on the fragile side. Fortunately, tailor-made storage options are easy to find.

There's nothing more frustrating than dealing with a tangle of Christmas lights. Quell the chaos with specially designed plastic spools that make it kind when you unwind. For a more inexpensive option, wrap them around a piece of heavy cardboard or a wrapping-paper tube.

Invest in an ornament chest with thick, stable dividers to keep dust and pests out but protection built right in. Got leftover tissue paper? Scrunch it up and use it to cushion the layers. If your ornaments are particularly valuable, either from an investment or sentimental perspective, consider an archival quality chest that's made from acid-free materials. Chests made of standard cardboard can cause discoloration and deterioration of your ornaments over the long haul.

Watch Out!

Keep your live tree watered. A dried-out Christmas tree is a major fire hazard, accounting for some 400 fires annually, according to the U.S. Fire Administration. A short in the electrical lights or a lighted candle nearby can ignite a dry tree in seconds. As a precaution, consider buying an automatic watering system. They're disguised as gift boxes and fit right under the tree.

Keep your most precious ornaments stored in their original packaging for the best protection. Food ornaments, like gingerbread cookies, should be double-sealed, first in plastic and then in a tin container to keep away pests with a sweet tooth.

Artificial wreaths and garlands keep their fresh-looking appearance and dust-free shapes longer when stored in boxes. Remove all wire and metal decorations before you pack them away. They could rust in high-humidity conditions. Another easy option is to hang wreaths on a wall of your basement or garage, then cover them up. It's also a good place to store holiday lawn ornaments.

Centralize all your wrapping paper and accessories. Upright plastic containers hold a season's worth of wrapping paper rolls without taking up much storage space. Other models are shaped to fit under a bed and are wide enough to hold gift boxes, too. Over-the-door hanging models have pouches to hold scissors, tape, ribbons, and bows.

For a Holly Jolly Christmas

One Santa wannabe says Christmas is part nostalgia, part fantasy for him. The sights and smells help to remind him of Christmases past—the people who've come and gone—while the newly added decorations give him something to look forward to for the following season.

Yet, experts say the holidays are the most stressful, anxiety-ridden time of year. There's so much to do, gifts to buy, parties to prepare, and every season, there's more pressure to surpass the year before. In some neighborhoods, decorating the home has turned into an extreme sport.

Word to the Wise

Want instant ambiance? Buy a DVD of a crackling fireplace and have it play in the background while you're decorating or entertaining. Some are so real you can practically feel the heat. You'll have all the charm of a Yule log with none of the ashes to clean up!

If you're the kind of person who'd rather enjoy a Christmas state of mind, instead of state of chaos, putting a storage system in place will do wonders for your private wonderland.

Put out only a few special items if the thought of doing a full-blown decorating redesign brings on an anxiety attack. Add some live strategically placed poinsettias and you'll cut down on your storage woes.

Once the holiday is over, concentrate on how you put things away. End-of-season inertia is often responsible for a slipshod get-it-over-with approach. Don't forget that nearly a full year will pass before you use these items again. If you don't do it right, next year will start off all wrong.

part 7

keep it up

Hopefully, by the time you reach this part of the book, you're well on your way to making your organized home a reality. Feels good, right? But there are a few more tips that we want to pass on to you. First, it's important to know that even if a house is organized, it will still look cluttered if it's not clean. So banish those dust bunnies to your (newly reorganized) trash bin. And, secondly, don't get discouraged. Organizing your home will always be a work in progress. But if you keep going and make sure that everything in your home has it's own place, you'll be well on your way to an organized present and future. Read on to learn more!

Chapter 20
Clean Up Your Act

CLEANING AND ORGANIZING ARE CLOSELY RELATED. It's difficult to clean until you've reduced your clutter (professional cleaners estimate that purging cuts cleaning time by 40 percent). After you've organized, cleaning brings that final polish to your home. Just as you've struggled to develop organizational strategies that will work over the long haul, you'll also want to develop cleaning strategies that are simple and effective and will work for years to come. This chapter will offer cleaning tips—from speed cleaning to green cleaning and everything in between.

Expect Imperfection

Perfectionism can be paralyzing, just as a willingness to embrace imperfection can be liberating. Cleaning is always a work in progress because life is messy—the more people and animals that share a space, the messier it becomes. One of the best ways to adapt yourself to this reality is to expect that you probably won't be able to achieve constant perfection on every front all the time.

Once you've been able to relax into this reality, you'll be better able to develop cleaning systems that will be adaptable to a variety of circumstances. You might want to think in terms of developing weekly (or even daily) rituals. You could either plan to run a load of laundry each day (if your situation warrants that) or you could plan to devote a day each week to the laundry. The FlyLady recommends that certain tasks be delegated to specific days—for example, you could plan to pay bills on Friday, do laundry on Saturday, and reserve vacuuming for Monday. This type of system can keep you from feeling overwhelmed, because you simply focus on the task that you've planned to do on a single day instead of feeling swamped by undone tasks and worrying about how to manage them all. This kind of system might also allow you to keep your home more consistently clean because you'll be rotating through the major weekly tasks instead of procrastinating for weeks on end on the projects that you find least desirable.

The Bottom Line

Mahatma Gandhi was able to embrace his weaknesses along with his strengths. He wrote, "My imperfections and failures are as much a blessing from God as my successes and my talents and I lay them both at his feet."

Whatever kind of cleaning system you adopt, allow for flexibility. Allow yourself to fail without becoming overly critical. Most people were never really taught to clean well—this is a skill that can be learned with time, patience, and persistence. Different phases of your life will place different demands on you, and sometimes you'll find yourself in a messier home. Just be realistic about what is possible within the confines of your own life, pace yourself, and continue to take steps toward your goals. Know that you'll surely hit obstacles along the way, but if you're not too daunted by imperfection, you'll be able to overcome them. A professional house cleaner offered this advice to Victoria Moran about cleaning: "You have to pretend you're cleaning someone else's house," she said. "Stack anything that hasn't been picked up. Don't read the magazine, answer the letter, or play with the Frisbee. Just stack the stuff and clean." She also said that the key to efficient housekeeping is to do the job "quickly, imperfectly, and without emotional investment."

Speed Cleaning

If you want to dramatically reduce the amount of time you spend cleaning, purchase the book *Speed Cleaning* by Jeff Campbell and the Clean Team. This book will show you how to move from room to room, tackling each part of the room only once. It will help you not only spend less time cleaning, but also to spend less money on cleaning products. You can also learn more about speed cleaning by visiting *www.thecleanteam.com.*

Here is a paraphrase of some of the helpful tips that can be found on the website:

- Work around the room one time—and one time only. Carry your equipment with you (in a pocketed apron, for example) so that you don't have to frequently interrupt your work to go searching for supplies.

- Begin at the top and work down. Because gravity pulls dirt and debris downward, it makes no sense to clean the floor before cleaning the counter. If you begin at the top and work down, you'll save precious time and energy.

- Skip clean spots. Don't become so invested in the work of cleaning that you clean surfaces that don't demand it. If you see just a few fingerprints or smudges, just wipe those down and ignore the rest.

- Keep moving. After an area is clean, do not continue to labor there. Your goal is to move as quickly as possible through the house, and lingering will slow you down.

- Use tools that really work. In some cases, you'll need to invest in heavier-duty tools to tackle tougher jobs. Keep all cleaning tools and supplies in good shape so that you won't waste time on leaky bottles, broken brooms, and vacuums that have lost their ability to pick up dirt effectively.

- Make sure you put your tools back in exactly the same spot each time. Otherwise, you'll lose time hunting for them.

- Be attentive to the work at hand and you'll be more successful.

- Pay attention to the amount of time it takes to speed clean your home and strive to get a little faster each time.

- Use both of your hands and you'll dramatically increase your speed. Finish one step with one hand and start the next job with the other.

With cleaning, there are many shortcuts you can take. Be creative about developing your own strategies for making the work fun and efficient. The FlyLady, for example, recommends that you learn to clean the tub while you're in it. She says that you can manage bathtub rings with just a little bit of soap on a washcloth. You might also consider adding baking soda to your bath and wiping the tub down afterward. Baking soda not only relaxes sore joints, but it is also a great, nontoxic, effective cleaner.

Embrace Baking Soda

Baking soda is a cheap, environmentally friendly alternative to harsher cleaners. It is so safe that you can use it on your teeth and in baking, but you can also use it to scour tiles, scrub toilets, remove the grime from sinks, get rid of odors in the refrigerator and on carpets, and wipe down your kitchen counters. This all-purpose household item is a great product to always have on hand.

Another way to reduce the amount of time you spend cleaning is to be attentive to dirt before it even enters your home. Purchase a high-quality doormat that is about function rather than aesthetics.

Remove Your Shoes

In many countries around the world, it is standard practice to remove shoes before entering a home, a temple, a church, or a mosque. In these contexts, keeping one's shoes on is considered a sign of great disrespect. In your home, you can reduce the amount of dirt and cleaning by leaving your shoes (and asking guests to leave their shoes) at the front door. Your hardwood floors and tiles will hold up better without rough shoes to contend with, and much carpet soiling can be avoided. Purchase some slip-on shoes for outdoor use (such as clogs or sandals) so that you can quickly slip your shoes off and on in a pinch.

Watch Out!

According to professional cleaners, as much as 85 percent of the dirt in your home comes from outside and has made its way in on the bottom of your shoes or in the paws of your pets. You can reduce exposure to lead dust by almost 60 percent if you wipe your shoes on a sturdy mat and leave them outdoors.

Not only is it practical from a cleaning perspective to keep one's shoes at the door, the dirt that comes into your home may actually pose a safety hazard. According to the Environmental Protection Agency (EPA), you can reduce exposure to lead dust by leaving your shoes outside. A report called the "Door Mat Study" presents the theory that soil that has been contaminated by lead causes almost all of the lead contamination inside your home. If you consistently leave your shoes outdoors, you may also be able to reduce your exposure to pesticides (from the lawn and garden), as well as industrial toxins, allergens, and dust mites.

If it feels inhospitable to you to ask guests to remove their shoes, keep in mind the Japanese custom of supplying guests with slippers to wear. The Japanese actually provide slippers at the door of the home, as well as separate slippers for use in the bathroom. Invest in slippers that are comfortable and aesthetically appealing, both for your own family and for your guests, and you'll likely have no trouble convincing them to leave their shoes at the door.

You might want to also supply guests with a visual cue—in some cases, a shoe rack beside the door will be enough to cue them to your custom of going shoeless indoors. In other situations, you might need to create a sign and hang it on your door, as Americans are not generally accustomed to removing their shoes every time they enter a home. Most guests will respect your policy, even if it feels a little awkward to you to ask them to remove their shoes.

Messy Pets

If you have pets, you know that as much as they enrich your life, they also generate a good deal of fur and soiling that must be dealt with. If you have a dog that sheds frequently, you can spend less time picking up hair if you devote just a few minutes each day to brushing the dog. Not only do most dogs relish the attention, but brushing the dog can be relaxing for the dog owner. Instead of being forced to pick up hair all over the house, most hair will be consolidated on the dog brush and can be immediately transferred to the garbage.

If you have trouble keeping up with cat hair, purchase a Zoom Groom, a rubber, massaging brush that cats love (after they get used to it). The

Zoom Groom will quickly and efficiently remove excess hair from your cat so that you will not need to be chasing hairballs all over the house.

You might consider giving your cat hairball-preventive treatments every week or every few days, depending on the length and condition of your cat's hair. This treatment will help prevent vomiting because of hairballs.

Cats also tend to track litter away from their litter box. If this is a problem with your cat, purchase a special mat at a pet-supply store. You might consider storing two litter boxes in the tub (one over the drain). By the time the cat has jumped out of the tub, litter has been shaken from his feet and you can easily sweep it up with a small brush.

Make It Fun

One of the best ways to increase your cleaning efficiency (and your efficiency in almost any area of life) is to find ways to enjoy the task. If you can find ways to transform cleaning from a chore into a game, you're halfway there. One time-tested pick-up game involves choosing a certain number of items, setting a timer, and racing against the clock to get these items picked up.

Race Against the Clock

Many people feel that this kind of game can make cleaning a lot more enjoyable and manageable. If you know you're going to set the timer and only clean for a designated amount of time, you're less likely to feel overwhelmed by the scope of the task. It is always easier to take on a five-minute project than it is to attempt to tackle a two-hour one. Another benefit of transforming cleaning into a game is that it is much easier to get children involved in a fun game or race than it is to try to get them involved in household "work."

Engage Your Kids

If you're tired of cleaning up after your kids, challenge them to join in. Visit any well-run preschool room and you'll see many ways that teachers integrate the work of cleaning into the school day. In some preschools, children sing a song as they clean. In others, children are just reminded to clean up after themselves after meals and snacks. While kids may balk at these kinds of directives at home, they generally obey their teachers because they understand from the beginning that cleaning is part of the arrangement.

If you want to make cleanup fun for your children, there are a few things to keep in mind. First, just as you need not (and should not) demand perfection from yourself in the domestic realm, don't expect perfection from your kids. Think of every cleaning effort on their part as "training" for them. If you encourage and point out the good work they're doing, they'll be more inclined to keep going. If you criticize and correct, they're likely to become discouraged and quit. Either ignore their failings so that they can develop a long-term positive association with cleaning or offer suggestions in an encouraging way, such as, "You're doing a great job folding the towels. Would you like me to show you how I roll socks?"

You can also get really creative with children and cleaning. Try making sock puppets for dusting and have a contest to see who can pick up the most dirt in a set amount of time. Or put on a CD and every time a song ends, switch to the next chore. Especially in your child's bedroom, allow him to take part in organizing the space in a way that is logical to him. If you always do the organizing for him, you may often find the room in chaos because the child does not understand your system. Help him develop his own kid-friendly systems. It's also a good idea to invest in kid-sized cleaning implements when children are small so that they can mimic you as you sweep, vacuum, and dust. This way, cleaning might feel less intimidating to them as they grow older.

Green Cleaning

Increasingly, people are searching for cleaning methods that are safe, cheap, and efficient. During pregnancy, especially, many women cannot tolerate the smell of many of the more toxic cleaners, such as bleach and oven cleaners. Although limited exposure to household cleaners may not cause harm to human health, nobody knows for sure what the threshold is. At what point do household cleaners become a threat to those who live in a home? Some studies suggest that certain people—such as children and the elderly—are more vulnerable to negative health impacts from household cleaners than are more resilient groups.

An Economical Choice

While organic foods typically cost more than "conventional" foods, this trend generally does not carry over into cleaning products. While purchasing ready-made natural cleaners at a health-food store may be more expensive than purchasing cleaning products at your local drugstore, there are many simple household items that are cheap to stock, easy to work with, and nontoxic. These items, which most people already have on hand, can assist you as you begin to explore green cleaning.

Watch Out!

If you use conventional house cleansers, never mix products—especially products containing bleach. Some people have actually died from the fumes created by their accidental toxic blends. Also, be sure to rinse well between products to prevent them from mingling. Be mindful as well that although baking soda is a gentle and safe cleaner, when it is combined with bleach, it becomes toxic. Never mix bleach with any chemical or "natural" cleaner.

Not only are these items cheaper than conventional household cleaners, it can be fun to "play the chemist" by mixing up your own green cleaners. A small amount of lavender oil or lemon can bring a fresh aroma to many of these cleaners. Experiment with these products until you find combinations that work for your home.

Here is a list of Green-Cleaning Products, as well as possible uses for each of them. This list comes from Robyn Griggs Lawrence's book *The Wabi-Sabi House: The Japanese Art of Imperfect Beauty*:

- **Olive oil:** Mix 3 parts oil to 1 part vinegar for a clean shine on your wooden furniture

- **Club soda:** Can be used to clean windows and give fixtures a shiny gleam

- **Vinegar:** Ideal for cleaning hardwood floors, and can be used to wipe down grease, diminish soap buildup, and deodorize

- **Borax:** Can kill mold and disinfect

- **Salt:** When mixed with water, this combination can kill bacteria

- **Baking soda:** Can be used to scour and remove odors, and can be combined with vinegar to clean stainless steel

If you clean the inside of your home with nontoxic products, you and your family might become healthier as well. The U.S. Environmental Protection Agency has determined that in many homes, levels of indoor pollution can be somewhere between two to five times higher than outdoor pollutants. Surprisingly, newer homes (those built after 1970) are at a greater risk for this problem because these homes tend to be better sealed against the elements than older homes. While these homes are generally more heat-efficient than their older counterparts, the tight seal on the windows and doors also prevents household toxins—not just those from cleansers, but also carbon monoxide from gas appliances—

from escaping. According to an article called "Healthier Indoor Air" by Aisha Ikramuddin in *The Green Guide #76*, well-sealed homes also give rise to dust mites and mold. "Whenever possible, ventilate," she writes. "Let your home breathe and you'll breathe better."

Do You Need a Hand?

As you become more realistic with yourself about your skills and capacities, consider hiring a cleaning person. This hiring does not have to be a substantial investment. You could hire a cleaning person to come just once a month, for example, or every other week. Even if you are on a tight budget, a cleaning person might still be in your budget if you can find ways to reduce your overall spending.

The cost of hiring a professional cleaning person varies a great deal depending on where you live. In a rural area, where the cost of living is generally lower than a larger city, you can expect to pay less than in a major urban area.

Word to the Wise

Victoria Moran on hiring a cleaning person: "Getting this kind of help is not self-indulgence. It is time management . . . I look at having her clean my house the way I look at having the dentist clean my teeth: I do the daily stuff; she does the deep cleaning."

Although everyone can develop cleaning skills and routines that work for them, certain situations may make hiring a cleaning person particularly useful. If you work from home, for example, you'll probably want your environment to be reasonably tidy. This will help you to better function as a professional. If you consistently struggle to balance your desire for a clean home with your work deadlines, you might hire somebody to help with the cleaning details. This person can tackle the weightier chores such as mopping and scrubbing out the tub, while you and your family work together to manage the lighter daily maintenance work.

Although cleaning is often thought of as a chore, it can be simplified, and in some cases even enjoyed, if you find a deeper meaning in the work. The more you strategize about cleaning solutions that will work for you, the more likely you are to feel involved in and challenged by the process. Cleaning does not just have to be about the final product, but the actual process can be good for you—cleansing your mind and giving you a break from the more abstract work that might be associated with your job. As Victoria Moran writes, "In the everyday maintenance of our homes, we have the option of experiencing peace, contentment, and that safe feeling of being part of something that is large and grand and good."

And remember, if you continue to take small steps each day to order your home and to make it beautiful, that feeling of peace and contentment will grow until it permeates the entire house.

Chapter 21

Finishing Touches

AS YOU'VE WORKED THROUGH THE CHAPTERS OF THIS BOOK, you've hopefully learned a great deal about what works for you in terms of organization. This final chapter will bring together some of the principles outlined in the book, as well as offer ideas about learning to manage the final frontier—your time.

The End of Yo-Yo Organizing

In Julie Morgenstern's book *Organizing from the Inside Out*, she coins the term "yo-yo organizing." This concept is similar to the yo-yo diet habit, where you try one diet after another, often with some temporary success, only to fail in the end. Just as yo-yo dieters often gain more weight than they lose, yo-yo organizers often tackle the clutter in their homes with zeal, only to eventually end up with more chaos and clutter than they began with.

The Bottom Line

The ideal solutions are those that wear well with time because they are realistic, are a good fit for your own preferences, personality, and lifestyle, and are flexible enough that they can be modified for each phase of life.

What goes wrong? Why do so many diets (and home-organization methods) fail? According to Morgenstern, the problem is that most of the books and methods focus on external solutions to problems that can only be solved internally. You cannot buy your way out of the chaos—organizational systems work only to the extent that the person who is using them has taken a customized approach to their unique situation, abilities, and personality.

Organizing Your Time

You might find that as you bring order to the different rooms in your home, you become aware of the less-tangible elements of your life—such as time management—that continue to be somewhat chaotic. It might be helpful to think of time as Julie Morgenstern does—in a very concrete way. Just as it is possible to tackle the chaos in your closets, it is equally possible to bring order to the hours of your day.

For Morganstern, time was the last thing she learned to organize. For her, the first steps were bringing order to her home, her purse, her office. Only after she found a way to manage the concrete details of these areas did she find the impetus to learn to organize her time. It was nothing short of a revelation for her to discover that organizing her time was just like organizing her closet. Her overstuffed closets were, in reality, finite spaces that could only contain a finite amount of clothing.

The first step was recognizing that time—although it might feel somewhat abstract in comparison to one's closet—is actually limited. Julie had packed her life so full that it was difficult to see what was important and to prioritize. It is hard to be efficient when you cannot see clearly the items or opportunities before you. Like her closets, Julie needed to peer at her life with open eyes and begin to reconsider the way she spent her time.

Just Say No

Just as managing and purging clutter is an essential first step as you seek to bring order to your home, learning to say "no" is an equally essential skill as you seek to organize your time. It is the fastest, most efficient way to declutter your day and reclaim your life. For some people, saying no can be difficult, but as you do it more and more, you experience the rewards—the gift of a streamlined, focused, and productive life—and saying no becomes as much of a healthy habit as the other ones mentioned in this book.

Word to the Wise

If you want to say no to something but fear you lack the courage, consider the possibility that the chaos in your home might be a direct result of an inability to say no. Sometimes people become so engaged with solving other people's problems that they neglect their own. This kind of neglect often shows up in chaotic homes.

Just as we do not recommend that you charge into your cluttered basement or attic without a plan, it might also be helpful to think of time in similar terms. As you struggle to divide your time between jobs, opportunities, and relationships, you might consider creating a criterion for weighing each option.

Sometimes, it can be helpful to consider whether a potential opportunity causes you more exhaustion or exhilaration than it's worth. Although a certain amount of exhaustion is inevitable, if you can say no to more of the opportunities that exhaust you and yes to more of the ones that exhilarate you, you will be happier and more productive.

Long-Term Goals

Another time-management essential is balancing your time between immediate concerns and long-term goals. In many situations, it can be tempting to constantly live as if you're putting out fires—just managing one urgent problem after another. But if you can begin to schedule time into your week to manage situations that are not yet pressing but will become increasingly urgent if ignored, you will simplify your life and gain greater peace of mind.

Create a To-Do List

You may find it helpful to sit down each morning with a notepad and pen and create a to-do list. This way you'll go into the day with a sense of purpose and priorities. Your list might include your personal and work-related objectives for the day. Or your list may include errands, meetings, appointments, phone calls to make, and e-mails to write. It should also include tasks that bring you closer to achieving your personal, professional, and financial long-term goals. After you create your to-do list, prioritize each task and input the appropriate information into your personal planner, PDA, or other scheduling tool. Ideally, you will plan out as much of your day as possible, leaving a realistic amount of time to deal with unexpected events.

Your to-do list can also keep your household organized and clean. For example, when you're about to embark on a massive cleanup or reorganization project, writing out a to-do list helps you clearly define your objectives, create a time frame, and take a well-thought-out approach to your efforts.

Create a Task List

For the day-to-day tasks that are necessary to run your home and keep it clean, follow these basic steps:

1. Create a list of what tasks you need to do (clean the bathroom, do the laundry, change bed linens, vacuum, wash the kitchen floor, go to the dry cleaner, mow the lawn, and so on).

2. Determine how often each of these tasks needs to be done.

3. Using a calendar, PDA, scheduler, or personal planner, create a schedule for accomplishing these tasks one at a time. For example, cleaning the bathroom may take thirty minutes after work on Mondays. Trips to the dry cleaner can be done on Tuesdays and Thursdays on the way to work or when dropping your kids off at soccer practice.

After you create a to-do list for keeping your home clean and organized, try to work through it one item at a time. Do not become discouraged if you get sidetracked—just pick up where you left off when you have the opportunity.

A Work in Progress

As you begin to better manage your home and time, keep in mind that many things are works in progress. Don't become distressed when things do not go as you'd hoped. As with any major project, there will be setbacks, failures, and unanticipated challenges. If you know that you will hit many bumps along the way, you will be less likely to let them deter you for any length of time.

Word to the Wise

As you develop your methods and slowly become more organized, you'll periodically want to assess your systems and see what is working and what isn't. Sometimes, something that worked well for several months will no longer work well. Be flexible with yourself, and modify your systems (and your goals) depending on the real circumstances you find yourself in.

As you begin to experience the rewards of a more ordered home and schedule, you might find that these aspects of your life become increasingly easy to maintain because they have built-in rewards. It feels good to have a sense of a reasonably ordered life, especially in the face of all of life's uncertainties.

Work Toward Your Goals

As you establish your long-term organizational goals, determine exactly what it will take to achieve each goal. Divide up each long-term goal into a series of short-term or medium-term goals that are more easily achievable. After you create a series of smaller goals, develop a timeline and set specific deadlines. Each time you accomplish one of these smaller goals, you'll be that much closer to achieving one of your long-term goals.

In your mind, you want to know clearly what you're working toward, how much time you have to achieve your objectives, and what possible rewards you can expect upon achieving your goals. You'll want to have a clear sense of why you're working toward a particular objective and what success in that area will mean to you.

Celebrate Success

After you've had an opportunity to develop some organizational skills and habits that work for you, remember to continue to pace yourself. Every domestic success should be celebrated. For most people, taking a few moments to celebrate success can be a helpful way to bring more joy to the work and to ultimately accomplish more.

It can be tempting to become so fixed on your goal that you never take a moment to rest and reflect on all that you've accomplished. Sometimes you might offer yourself incentives such as, "I'll clean out this drawer and then take a break with a cup of coffee," only to find that you get so involved with the work of organizing that you forget about your reward. This kind of approach can cause burnout over the long haul.

Especially when you're faced with a major organizational task, you don't want to have memories of days and days of tackling the clutter in your garage with no break. If the work seems like drudgery, you're likely to procrastinate until it becomes unmanageable. If you take small steps and celebrate each success, you'll have a natural incentive to retain your organizational zeal over the years, when different organizational challenges (a new baby, a move, a death in the family) present themselves to you.

Stay Focused

Victoria Moran mentions a friend who, after wiping out her tub, said, "This is the most *real* thing I've done all day." Often, people postpone or dread housework simply because it seems like a waste of time when there are other, seemingly more important, things to do.

Word to the Wise

Victoria Moran writes, "In the landscape of our lives, making a home is front and center. The consensus of every major religion—and the majority of people who consider themselves happy—is that the primary tasks of humans is to learn how to love. . . . At home, with pretenses hung in the closet next to the business suits, we learn it best."

The truth is that the concrete realities of daily life are an essential part of being human, and these simple, manageable tasks, against the backdrop of a seemingly chaotic and unmanageable world, can be comforting to your soul.

Take Each Day as It Comes

Knowing that you're returning to an orderly home is a little bit like knowing that you're about to go on vacation—only in this situation, your home becomes your refuge. You don't need to pack and you don't need to spend any money, but you will experience the refreshment and relaxation you need to thrive.

Organizing your home and time are two pieces of the larger project of life—and they will always be works in progress—always involving difficult decisions, and finite resources. The pinch is felt especially when you have small kids, pets, and frequent houseguests. All of these little "distractions" are part of the package—because they help you to be more realistic, to realize what is essential. As Lin Yutang said, "Beside the noble art of getting things done, there is the noble art of leaving things undone. The wisdom of life consists in the elimination of nonessentials."

Glossary

archival quality: Conservation materials and techniques used in the preservation and storage of rare and old materials.

armoire: A tall cabinet, usually with drawers, shelves, and doors, used for storing clothes or household items.

baker's rack: A display unit, often made of iron, steel, or copper, that can serve as either decoration or as a functional piece for storage.

captain's bed: A bed frame that accommodates a mattress, without a box spring, and features working drawers for storage within the frame.

clutter: A confusing or disorderly state.

Clutterers Anonymous: A twelve-step recovery program that offers help to the true clutterer, who is overwhelmed by disorder.

conservator: An individual who cares for, restores, and repairs collectible objects.

consignment sale: An arrangement in which merchandise is sold by an agent on the seller's behalf.

cosmeceutical: A term coined by the cosmetic industry that refers to cosmetic products that have medicinal or therapeutic effects on the body.

crawl space: The space between the ground and the first floor of a home, usually no more than a few feet high.

data (memory) card/Memory Stick: A device used to store data for digital cameras, camcorders, and computers. The Memory Stick is a proprietary Sony product and it is used by nearly all of Sony's products that use flash media.

dead storage: Storage reserved for items that are no longer needed for immediate use but that are still required for records.

digital: The method of storing, processing, and transmitting information through the use of distinct electronic or optical pulses that represent the binary digits 0 and 1.

digital video recorder (DVR): A device that enables you to record and time-shift TV programs on a hard-disk drive for later viewing. Also known as personal video recorder.

DVD: A high-density compact disc used for storing large amounts of data, especially high-resolution audiovisual material.

eBay: An online shopping site with more than 100 million registered members from around the world.

ephemera: Documents published with a short intended lifetime.

external Zip disk drive: A removable disk storage system.

feng shui: An ancient Chinese practice of living harmoniously with the natural elements and forces of the Earth.

flexispace: A space or room in the home that can be utilized for any function as needed

Freecycle Network (*www.freecycle .org*): An online grassroots organization made up of communities around the globe that allows individuals to recycle their no-longer-wanted goods by offering them free to members.

garage system: A complete garage organization and storage plan.

home theater: A system of sophisticated electronic equipment for the presentation of theater-quality images and sound in the home.

International Association of Professional Organizers: An organization dedicated to setting and maintaining standards of excellence for professional organizers worldwide.

lazy Susan: A revolving tray typically used in the kitchen for condiments or food.

loft bed: A bunk bed in which the top of the mattress is more than 3 feet from the floor. Loft bunk beds, like other bunks, save space and add a creative element to a bedroom.

modular furniture: Furniture made up of independent units that can be combined into flexible formations.

mudroom: An anteroom to the house that provides a waterproof and weatherproof place for the removal and storage of rain or snow-covered clothes.

Murphy bed: A space-saving bed that folds up into a closet.

National Association of Professional Organizers (NAPO): A nonprofit organization of organizing consultants, speakers, trainers, authors, and manufacturers of organizing products. Founded in 1985, NAPO is the largest national association of and for organizers.

niche: A recess in a wall (may be used to house decorative objects).

obsessive-compulsive disorder (OCD): A neurobiological disorder characterized by recurrent, unwelcome thoughts and repetitive behavior.

online photo service: A website that provides users with the ability to print, enhance, archive, and store digital images. Popular sites are KodakGallery.com, Shutterfly.com, and Snapfish.com.

organic gardening: A method of gardening that uses only materials derived from living things, such as compost and manure for fertilization and pest control. In contrast to conventional gardening, the organic approach uses no synthetic chemicals at all.

pegboard: A board perforated with regularly spaced holes into which pegs can be fitted that allow for hanging storage of tools and other accessories.

personal video recorder (PVR): A device that enables you to record and time-shift TV programs on a hard-disc drive for later viewing. Also known as digital video recorder.

pocket door: A door that disappears into a specially built wall cavity.

PODS: Portable on Demand Storage

potting bench: A workspace and storage holder typically used by gardeners to pot or transplant plant material.

professional organizer: An individual who designs systems and processes using organizing principles to help clients take control of their homes and lifestyles.

purge housecleaning: The act of cleaning the rooms and furnishings of a house.

repurpose: Using an item for a different situation than was originally intended by the creator or manufacturer.

rewritable CD: A compact disc that allows users to read, write, and erase data.

R-value: A measure that indicates how well insulation resists heat flow. The higher the R-value, the better the insulation.

scanner: A machine that optically analyzes a two- or three-dimensional image and digitally encodes it for storage in a computer file.

self-storage facility: A property designed and used for leasing individual storage spaces. Charges are determined by the size of the room, per month.

shed: A building that is separate from a main building and usually used for storage.

thrift shop: A shop that sells secondhand goods at reduced prices.

ultraviolet light: Light lying outside the visible spectrum. The primary source of ultraviolet light is the sun. Ultraviolet rays can cause fading of paint finishes, carpets, photographs, art, and fabrics.

vertical space: The space above the head and high along the walls. Utilizing vertical space is an important element of storage planning.

window film: A protective coating designed to reduce the amount of solar heat transmission through window glass and prevent fading of furniture, artwork, and fabrics.